SEX & LOVE & ROCK&:

'Fired and inspiring.' John Heg

'"Too much poetry speaks to tᴏᴏ ᴧᴇw people', but Tony Walsh's poetry speaks to the many. In SEX & LOVE & ROCK&ROLL, words leap off the page: urgent and immediate, like his poetry performances. They tell us how it feels when the needle goes in, / when the bass, when the bass, when the bass, when the bass...' Helen Mort, award-winning poet.

'Tony turns the ordinary into the extraordinary. He effortlessly reveals the unseen, makes heroes of the has-been, helps find the lost and forgotten scraps of society and makes the world accessible to 'you' and to 'me' with his passionate and poignant Rock&Roll badland ballads.' Dan Cockrill, poet and host of Bang Said The Gun, London.

'Tony Walsh's free-wheeling poetic sensibility is grounded in the grit and glory of down-town jiggery and profound musicality. Here is a soul-scape panorama, horizon deep and breath-taking. Heart-warming and heart breaking, allowing you into the tender catacombs of a lived and loved life story. There is so much at work here. A big journey from a big man. Wonderful! A wizard of us. A red brick road you just gotta follow.' Gerry Potter, poet and playwright.

'Tony's rhyme and reasoning resonates with a bass from your heart strings. Northern souls – he knows us. The women in his poems have been sketched with empathy and celebration, their faltering described with emphatic passion, helplessness and love.' Cathy Crabb, award -winning playwright and performer.

'A lovely book; the whole thing sings.' AF Harrold, poet and author.

PRAISE FOR TONY WALSH

'Some poets can make you laugh, a few can make you cry but only a handful can do both. By all accounts, Tony Walsh is one such poet. Splitting your sides and breaking your heart? Be warned – this guy should come with a health warning!' Poetry&Words, Glastonbury Festival. (Website Poet In Residence 2011)

'Go Tony. The world's your oyster. This means that an oyster is the world. You rock!' Lemn Sissay MBE. Poet and playwright.

'A towering talent on the performance poetry scene, Tony blends native Manchester wit with a humanitarian heart to create moving and exhilarating poems.' Apples & Snakes.

'Tony Walsh's poetry picks you up by the scruff of the neck and shakes you until your teeth rattle. Brilliant stuff!' Felix Dennis - poet, publisher, Oz trial defendant.

'... Billy Bragg-like persona crossed with John Cooper Clarke delivery... The Fly is a music magazine, for sure, but in Tony Walsh's lone voice, we discover more music than a thousand orchestras could muster. Utterly mesmerising and unforgettable..." Stephen Brolan, The Fly, The Big Chill Festival review, 2009.

'Tony Walsh rocks. And indeed he rolls!' Elvis McGonagall, UK and World Poetry Slam Champion 2006.

'Glastonbury comes to StAnza... in the shape of the inimitable Tony Walsh... one of the UK's leading voices in performance poetry and a radio and festival regular." StAnza, Scotland's International Poetry Festival.

'(One) of the UK's finest performers... fast funny and humane poetry...' Ledbury Poetry Festival.

'...shamelessly populist and swaggeringly ambitious.' WhatsOnStage.com

'Masterful and empowering, a people's champion of poets... Tony speaks to the heart of the nation with a Manchester twang and a touch of indie wildness.' Conwy Feast.

'Tony Walsh emits charisma the way an AK47 emits rounds. It is physically impossible for a sentient human being to remain indifferent within a mile radius when he's on stage.' thelunecyreview.wordpress.com

'You could have heard a pin drop. As moving a theatre experience as you can imagine.' Eric Allison, Prisons Columnist for The Guardian.

'Tony Walsh jest jednym z najbardziej obiecujacych talentów sceny slamowej w Wielkiej Brytanii.' The British Council, Poland.

'Longfella did a great job.' Dan Walker of BBC Sport via Twitter
'Brilliant!' The National Football museum via Twitter
'Fabulous stuff...' Irvine Welsh via Twitter
(All referring to a poem commissioned by BBC1 Football Focus, January 2012.)

'There is formal skill from Tony Walsh...' Carol Ann Duffy, UK Poet Laureate.

'Our audience loved him and you will too!' Wicked Words, Leeds.

Tony Walsh was born in 1965, where the industrial outskirts of east Manchester huddle in the shadow of the Pennines. The oldest of four children born to an Irish father and an English mother, he was seriously ill with rheumatic fever as an infant and grew up in a 1930s council house.

After dropping out of University and spending 18 months unemployed in the mid-1980s, he worked in an industrial bakery, a sausage factory and as a Post Office counter clerk until being tied up at gun-point in an armed robbery in 1991.

Re-training as a Housing Officer in the most deprived parts of North Manchester, his home throughout the 90s, he then managed housing and community projects across mainly inner-city Manchester and Salford for nearly twenty years.

A writer of poetry since the age of five, he read at his first open mic event in Manchester in 2004, performed at Glastonbury Festival the following year, and became a full-time writer in 2011. 'Longfella' is a reference to his height of 6 feet 5.

An avid music fan, he began hanging around the stage door of Manchester post-punk gigs in 1979, sharing a can of McEwan's with The Jam's Paul Weller when aged just 14. He's been hanging around local music, poetry and fringe events ever since and is a featured artist in the Manchester District Music Archive.

Tony still lives in Greater Manchester with Helen, his wife and partner of nearly 30 years, and their teenage children, Joe and Katie. He performs his poetry at literary and music festivals around the UK and beyond, and leads acclaimed workshops in schools, colleges, universities and prisons. His work has been commissioned by BBC television and radio, published in magazines and anthologies in both the UK and USA, and translated into Russian.

'SEX & LOVE & ROCK&ROLL' is his first full collection.

www.longfella.co.uk @LongfellaPoet #SXLRR

TONY WALSH

SEX & LOVE & ROCK&ROLL

To Fiona,
Take This Pen!
Tony Walsh

longfella

Burning Eye

This edition published by Burning Eye Books 2013

www.burningeye.co.uk

@burningeye

Burning Eye Books
15 West Hill, Portishead, BS20 6LG

ISBN 978 1 90913 616 8

*In putting this book together, special thanks must go to Clive Birnie at
Burning Eye, to Mike Black for photography and to Dave Kirkwood
for his cover design and much more.*

For Queenie
For Elaine and Frank
For believing in me

For all my family and friends
For all my funders and followers
For supporting me

For Helen
For Joe and Katie
For putting up with me

For years

For you, dear reader
For buying books
For the love of them

Thank you

WARNING: the following poems may contain flashing images

CONTENTS

Introduction: A Manifesto	11
Too Much Poetry	19
Haiku	20
The Poetry Slam Prayer	21
Start All The Clocks	24
Sonnet Boom	27
Englishman/Irishman	30
Posh Things	31
Drunkle	32
Favourite Uncle	33
Under The Stairs	34
Haiku	36
A Girl, Like, Y'know	37
Nowhere Man	38
Haiku	40
Drastic Surgery	43
It's All Going Posh Down The Precinct	47
No Money	48
No Walls	49
Debris	50
Saving Deposits	52
No Mark	53
Found	55
Tiny Dreams	56
Someone	59
Going Nowhere	60
Haiku	61
Ho! Ho! Ho!	62
Haiku	64
Lover's Lament	65
Spangles	66
Battered	67
www.walnutwhipped.co.uk	68
Someone Warm To Hold	70
Intimacy	72
I Can Write A Rainbow	73
Bohemian Raspberry	75
Three Wishes	78
Let's Make A Love	79
Haiku	84
Nothing New	85
Cake Hole	87
Happy Meals	89
Haiku	90
Small Elephants	91

Stuck At The Lights	92
Haiku	93
Mother's Day	94
Haiku	96
Haiku	98
She Never	99
Flammable	100
Kept In The Dark	101
Haiku	102
Not Knowing	103
Sometimes	104
Haiku	106
Phish Out Of Water	107
Haiku	108
Tattooed Tigers	109
Don't Waste Your Breath	110
Bop 'Til You Drop	112
Smoke Lonely	113
Haiku	115
Cherry Blossom	116
Always There	117
Haiku	119
Hollow	120
Life Goes On	121
Haiku	122
Scrolling	123
Special Place	126
Rock&Roll	128
Keeping It Peel: Teenage Kicker Conspiracy	131
When Kendal Calls	132
Why Glastonbury	134
Black Jehovah	135
Haiku	138
Trash Planet	140
T-Shirt Philosophy	142
Sugar Spun Tornadoes	143
Neat Lawns (Now Watch This Drive)	145
Repeat After Me	147
Because The Poets Know	149
The Highest Hill	151
Take This Pen	152
The Last Gang In Town?	157
Notes	160

A MANIFESTO

'I don't know much about music;
in my line of work you don't have to.'
Elvis Presley

I've written poetry from the age of five, when my Nana, Queenie, would transcribe my earliest efforts into a treasured 1960s-styled notebook, using a red pen to write on its long, pink pages. It was at my Nan's also, aged 14 in 1979, listening in bed to John Peel's late night radio show on a tiny, tinny transistor radio, that I first heard Sonny's Lettah (Anti-Sus Poem) by Jamaican dub poet, Linton Kwesi Johnson. Packing a huge political, cultural and emotional punch, it hit me in the gut as hard as any piece of art has before or since. Together with the snap, crackle and be-bop-Beasley Street-cred of local hero, John Cooper Clarke, who knew that poetry could even do that? Could even be like that? Fucking wow!

As a music-mad kid, my first poets came disguised as lyricists: initially the likes of Paul Weller, Joe Strummer and Elvis Costello, but later along came Morrissey, Billy Bragg, Shane McGowan, Ian Dury, Johnny Cash, Chuck D, Eric Bogle, Ewan MacColl, Mark E Smith, Bob Marley, Tracey Thorne, Terry Hall, Michael Franti, Christy Moore, Smokey Robinson, Gil Scott Heron, Steve Earle, Patti Smith, Jarvis Cocker and a thousand other bedsit balladeers and manic street preachers. It took me a few years to work my way past the great punk myth that 1976 was a musical Year Zero, but I delved my way backwards: through Manchester's northern soul sounds into Motown, funk and blues; back through Two Tone and ska into dub and dancehall reggae; back from The Pogues into Irish and other folk musics; and back to the Hit Parades of the 50s, 60s and 70s, developing an appreciation of the (deceptively) simple, direct, affecting pop lyric. The early rappers – politicised and afro-centric, the terrace anthems of the Manchester scene, and the hands-in-the-air euphoria of the dance revolution all touched me deeply. The words and the music of the piece, working together to make you feel something. Folk music, all of it. Story telling. Connecting us. Mattering.

So when, in 2002/03, I wrote my first poems since my teens, now with a few of life's bruises, two small children and a terminally ill mother, this was my frame of reference. Not avant-garde or avant-meaning, avant-engagement, avant-got-a-clue-wot-you're-on-about-mate, stuff. But poetry that might hopefully get a hearing in the streets and pubs of my home town; poetry that would perhaps command the attention of music, comedy or theatre audiences; and poetry that could maybe, just maybe, change the mind of people expecting to be bored rigid. Often tightly rhymed and musically metred - we live our life to rhythms and patterns, we're hard-wired to receive them - but always trying to find a pulse or a heartbeat of some sort. Poems for the milkman to whistle; to make him laugh and cry when he caught the words.

So when I first wandered nervously into Manchester to stutter my stuff in packed, tiny rooms above old-school boozers, I was thrilled to find that there were people who got my reference points and shared my frustrations; plus great local poets, rising out of the local open mic scene onto national and international stages, who would further inform and inspire my hopes of what poetry could be. Should be. What it once was and can be again.

Giving truth to the cliché, I'd found male and female, young and old, gay and straight, black and white, the skint and the solvent; poets of all shapes and surprises - sharing their stories, telling their truths and, mercifully, miraculously, minded to muse momentarily on me mumbling mine.

From under hoods and hijabs I heard them. From under fringes and 'fros, buzzcuts and bobs, from under green hair and grey, moptops and Mohawks, dreadlocks and... dreadful haircuts of all styles and none, I heard them. Shouting quietly, whispering loudly; killing me softly with - their poems. I'd found orators, creators and innovators whose dazzling diction and eclectic, electric rhetoric simply demanded my attention. A folk poetry, all of it. Story telling. Connecting us. Mattering.

Not here, the classical curricular canon of Shakespeare and Co. Not here, the freeform word-jazz of the pre-post-avant-neo-quasi-ExҎeЯi-M3nTaLi5t$. Not here even the so-called mainstream poetry which, sadly, is only mainstream if you mainly stream it from the private lakes and remote backwaters of our culture, causing barely a ripple outside of its own talent pool. Icy to those who might dare dip a toe. Not drowning, but not waving either.

No, not here. Here was... something else.

To my life-changing delight, I'd stumbled across a poetry as ancient as it is modern. A poetry that, whether knowingly or not, is rooted in the age-old traditions and folk memories that pre-date the written word. A vibrant, exciting poetry that borrows knowingly from hip-hop, reggae, punk and folk; that draws skillfully from theatre and stand-up comedy as well as from traditional poetic forms and techniques; that learns equally from the sacred and the profane, from the saucy postcard and the gospel hymn, from the fire and brimstone preacher, from pop culture and from the cultures of many lands. I'd found a poetry of patois, Punjabi and Polari; of jingles, jazz and jive; of minstrels, monologues and music halls. I'd found tub thumping, tongue twisting, truth telling troubadours; bombastic beat-boxing broadside balladeers; slam-tastic street corner soapbox slang slingers. I found an accessible, democratic People's Theatre, no less; unashamed to wear the masks of both comedy and tragedy, eschewing those of bafflement, boredom and blatantly bogus bourgeois belonging which are worn at all-too-many a poetry reading. Inclusive, not exclusive; fun, not funereal; sexy not sexless. Intelligent not unintelligible. But who knew that poetry could even do that? Could even be like that. Fucking wow!

So good luck, I say, to those who wish to continue wandering lonely as a cloud, my respect even. Just please don't presume to claim the whole art form as yours and yours alone. Other poetics are also available.

Here, sugaring 'the P word', re-branded as 'performance poetry', 'slam poetry', 'stand-up poetry', 'spoken word' and 'live literature', here were poetry events and poets, single poems even, that can take black consciousness, pink power, blue jokes and a green manifesto and wrap it all up in a red flag emblazoned with the golden words: *if we can't fucking dance it's not our revolution!* Marching fearlessly and unapologetically towards the true mainstream of our culture, ready to tattoo the hearts of anyone who will listen. 'Oi, Emperor! We can see your arse, mate!' We Have Come. To Spread. The Word!

Quiet girls turned Riot Grrrls. Bard to the bone. Poetry will never be 'the new rock and roll', they'll tell you, because it will always be the original rock and roll! 'Mad, bad and dangerous to know', they'll tell you. 'Peace and love'. 'Fight The Power'. Punk as fuck, even when disguised as *librarians. (*Especially when disguised as librarians).

Put simply, I'd found what I wanted to do with the rest of my life, what I have to do with the rest of my life. And, here I am, a few short years on from that first open mic night; I've given up a good day job, run away with the circus and I'm presenting many of my poems here on the page for the very first time. If I'm honest, feeling more nervous and naked now than before any crowd, any classroom, any camera. I'm a 'performance poet', after all. It's the way I tell 'em, or so the dogma goes.

However, I've been lucky enough to have been invited to poetry, literary and arts events of all kinds in recent years. I've witnessed many, and read too few, of the finest poets from the UK, North America and around the world. I've been privileged to study their forms and techniques, and observe their stage-craft and lack of it at close hand. But I still have so much to learn, there's nothing to be gained from ignorance or inverse snobbery. I take no misguided pride therefore in my own limited poetic apprenticeship; we should always remain as students. Indeed, along the way I've learned that many 'stage poets' could learn a lot in terms of craft and artistry from the best 'page poets' and vice versa in terms of connection and presentation, thereby making the whole art form stronger, growing the scene, widening and connecting the audiences.

Ultimately I've learned that it's not about classical versus contemporary poetry, it's not about page versus stage, it's not about the raucous poetry slam versus the hushed reading, it's not about rhyme versus free verse, north versus south, or verses versus anything. Yes, there remain issues (count 'em!) around class, race, age, disability, gender and sexuality in the arts, as in so many walks of life. But, Jeez, I don't see anyone in our culture 'kicking against the pricks' harder or with more laser-guided, armour piercing wit and accuracy than our most socially engaged poets.

For me it's about communication – between poets, between poetries, with other artists and with new and strengthened audiences. It's about passion. It's about honesty. It's about the pursuit of truth and beauty. It's about poetry moving us to tears not boring us to tears. It's about entertainment value being admired not sneered at. It's about stopping attempts to reconcile the irreconcilable, stopping looking inwards, stopping the apologies for our art form and raising our game. It's about adopting the production values that modern audiences expect, reaching out to people young and old, and it's about 'most poetry ignoring most people' no longer. And it's about time.

So never mind the bollocks. Look up some of the poets and links listed at the back of this book, get along to a local poetry night, and if there isn't one – or if you think that it's shit – then start your own. The internet means that it's never been easier to find great stuff, to connect with the people and scenes that interest you, to study your craft, study your craft, study your craft and to get your own stuff out there. You don't need anyone's permission. You don't need to find your path blocked by self-appointed and increasingly irrelevant gatekeepers – just go around them. You don't even need to know where you're heading, where this thing might take you, or what the so-called rules are.

You just need a pen, a page and a passion.

So thank you for reading. I hope that you find a few lines here to make you smile, to make you cry, to make you think. To make you write, even.

These are my poems. Other poems are also available.

Tony Walsh | Longfella | February 2013

*'Most people ignore most poetry because
most poetry ignores most people.'*
Adrian Mitchell

TOO MUCH POETRY

SPEAKS TO TOO FEW PEOPLE.

Most, therefore, do not even begin to read. Or to listen.

Some try, but gain little for their efforts.

A few persevere, but find only pretension and

that, as with The Emperor's New Poems,

that there is neither meaning nor

even an engaging use of words,

sounds or images.

Understandably,

such people

come to the

conclusion

that poetry

isn't

really

worth

it.

Her poetry was
self-indulgent bollocks, but
they smiled and they clapped.

He read his poems
for an hour without once
communicating.

They laughed and they cried.
Her simple words, delivered
magnificently.

THE POETRY SLAM PRAYER

Let us pray.

Oh, Holy Gods of Slam
(Oh, Holy Gods of Slam)

Please bless
(Please bless)

Tonight's judges with wisdom
(Tonight's judges with wisdom)

Please ensure
(Please ensure)

That tonight's audience members
(That tonight's audience members)

Are well endowed
(Are well endowed!?)

With clapping, cheering and whooping
(With clapping, cheering and whooping)

Tonight we beseech you
(Tonight we beseech you)

That the poets are fearless
(That the poets are fearless)

That the poets are magnificent
(That the poets are magnificent)

That the poets are not shit!
(That the poets are not shit!)

Oh, Holy Gods of Slam
Tonight we pray...

Bring us nail biting tale writing!
Bring us ground breaking sound making!
Bring us heart stopping, chart topping,
page ripping, stage gripping,
hard shoving, bard loving,
loud speaking, crowd freaking,
eye popping, cry stopping,
chest pounding, best sounding,
pride spitting, side splitting,
tears stinging, ears ringing words!

Bring us fist shaking risk taking!
Bring us long lasting tongue blasting!
Bring us race winning, face grinning,
brain shifting, pain lifting,
truth teaching, youth reaching,
goal setting, go getting,
great learning, hate spurning,
speed dating, greed hating,
blind seeing, mind freeing,
tub thumping, blood pumping words!

Bring us street fighting greased lightning!
Bring us shock jocking block rocking!
Bring us scene stealing, dream feeling,
hole filling, soul thrilling,
life changing, wide ranging,
worth waiting, earth quaking,
jaw dropping, war stopping,
peace-making, piss taking,
fool hounding, cool sounding,
star turning, bra burning,
grrrl powering, world flowering,
queer saving, fear braving,
trail blazing, whale saving,
tree hugging, free loving,
beat missing, sweet kissing,

lip slinging, hip swinging,
un-zipping, fun stripping,
shit kicking, clit licking,
good looking, love fucking
POETRY!

Amen!
(Amen!)

START ALL THE CLOCKS

Start all the clocks

One stage
One microphone
One poet

One brain
One mouth
One human soul

One audience
One spotlight
One hundred and eighty seconds

Slam poetry? (Tickticktickticktickticktick)
Tell me about it...

Tell me how it feels when you fight from the womb
To the light and delight in a brightly lit room

Or tell me how it feels when your mother baked cakes
All the butter and sugar and love that it takes

Or tell me how it feels when you play on the swings
When you blow out the candles and everyone sings

Or tell me how it feels on your first day at school
When your Mam cut your fringe and your mittens were cool

Or tell me how it feels as you run in the sand
With a bucket and spade and your Dad holding hands

Or tell me how it feels when your Dad... moves away
To a ready-made family. And what did he say?

Tell me about it

Or tell me how it feels when you score and you're proud
And they think it's all over but, no! Disallowed!

Or tell me how it feels when you start to grow breasts
When Mother Nature writes 'woman' across a girl's chest

Or tell me how it feels when you walk down the aisle
With your father in tears as your step-mother smiles

Or tell me how it feels when you look in his eyes
And when *you* know that *he* knows that *you* know it's *lies*

Or tell me how it feels when a boy racer crashes
When Mum has to scatter her boy's wasted ashes

Or tell me how it feels when the needle goes in
When the bass, when the bass, when the bass, when the bass,
when the bass, when the bass, when the bassline kicks in

Tell me about it

Or tell me how it feels when there *is no* blue line
On the pregnancy test for the seventeenth time

And tell me how it feels when that splits up your marriage
And then you get pregnant. And then you miscarriage

Or tell me how it feels to be judged by your race
When your kids have to watch as he spits in your face

Or tell me how it feels when you're kicked from beneath
When you're spitting out blood, snot and fury and teeth

Or tell me how it feels when you mark out the line
That 'enough is enough is enough *it's my time!*'

Or tell me how it feels to fight back from bereavement
To use it as fuel for a life of achievement

Tell me about it

Or tell me how it feels when you're crossing the line
In a personal best and a world record time

Or tell me how it feels to *defy* your oppressors
To look back with pride at a life of successes

Or tell me how it feels when you've shattered the odds
When you've thrown off their shackles and danced with the gods

Or tell me how it feels when you're slamming it, do you
Fill holes in their souls? Do they shout hallelujah?

Or tell me how it feels to slam all of the doom...
And the gloom from a room... and commune us as humans

And tell me how it feels... to deliver... a line...
That everyone... hangs on... How words can ... stop time

And tell me how it feels when you finish and then
People laughing and crying and the judge holds up... 6.4!?

(Six? Point Four?? What the...?)

Slam poetry?
Tell me about it!

Stop all the clocks

SONNET BOOM

They told me I should use a classic form
to prove that I'm a master of my craft.
'A sonnet would go down a fucking storm!'
'A sonnet? Me!? You're joking! Don't be daft!'

They said that, as a poet versed in rhyme,
a sonnet would be well within my reach.
They said that I should allocate the time
to learn the form and all it has to teach.

So then they showed me how a sonnet goes;
in fourteen lines; three fours and then a two.
And then they stressed about iambic flows,
pentameter of ten beats, five times two.

They said the final twist is sure to come.
De-dum, de-dum, de-dum, de-dum, de-dum.

'Be nice to your children. They may grow up to be writers.'
Katerina Stoykova Klemer

ENGLISHMAN / IRISHMAN

It was the 1970s.

And as a small boy growing up in England
I would often tell Englishman, Irishman, Scotsman jokes
to my Irish father.
Taking a childish delight in
the Irishman as the thick one,
the stupid one,
the smelly one.

It was the 1970s.

My father never laughed,
but sometimes a smile would betray him.
Not for the joke.
But for the small boy,
untroubled
in his eagerness to please.

If I hurt his feelings
I never felt his hurt.
He never *said* anything.

It was the 1970s.

POSH THINGS

Posh things:
Like in the catalogue and on the telly.
Like fridges and telephones.
Like visitors and watching BBC.

Posh things:
Like brown bread and plain milk.
Like strange fruit and vegetables.
Like tinned peaches and Battenburg cake.

Posh things:
Like Milk Tray and The Pop Man.
Like long matches and onyx ashtrays.
Like flowers and dentists.

Posh things:
Like football games and fairground rides.
Like banks and libraries.
Like holidays and trips – to Stockport.

Posh things:
Like neat gardens and trained dogs.
Like spare rooms and spare change.
Like fitted carpets and soft towels.

Posh things:
Like… somewhere to go and… going there.
Like… wanting stuff and getting stuff.
Like… knowing stuff and… doing stuff.

Posh things; like *paying* for your school dinners. And leaving some.
Posh things; like new clothes and barber shops.
Posh things; like warm rooms and dry walls.
Posh things; like not lying and not needing to.
Posh things; like *fucking confidence and That. Fucking. Look.*

Posh things.
              Like fathers.
                          And quietness.

31

DRUNKLE

He was our drunken
Uncle James.

But we all called him

Drunkle Jimmy.

When he wasn't there.

Which was more often than not.

We told our cousin, but she

never laughed.

FAVOURITE UNCLE

He *was*
my favourite uncle.

Cool.
More like a mate.
He brought me candy bars from Zanzibar
and everything was great.
He told me 'bout a place
in outer space and *said* he'd take me there.
He bought me sherbert dips and walnut whips.
He answered *all* my prayers.

He gave me building blocks.

And Batman socks.

And called me

'our kid'.

But he fell out

with me Mam

and left.

Like all the others did.

UNDER THE STAIRS

Forgotten things. Unwanted things.
And things *used* every day.

Mr Muscle and Baby Bio.
Mr Muscle and Miracle-Gro.
Stuff for dirty laundry and
stuff for dirty hands.

Brushes – used and abandoned.
Rolls for papered cracks.
Dribbled tins and splattered tins
and tell-tale signs on sticks.
Scarlet Blush, Angel's Tears, Virgin White.

A steam iron.
To crease and to flatten and to scald and to press-ssss
ssShhhhhh-oe polish – oxblood and cherry red.
Black and blue and brown and pink.

Six of the finest garden canes.
Turpentine and gloss.
Sprays for bugs and slugs and flies
and bleach and polish and whitewash.
Stain remover and scratch remover and
nails and No More Nails. And
One. Small. Child.

Never more alone.

A whole cathedral's 'worth' of candles. 'Saved'.
Still wick'ed in the shadows.

Forgotten things. Unwanted things.
And things *used* every day.

Mr Muscle and Baby Bio.
Mr Muscle and Miracle-Gro.
Stuff for dirty laundry and

stuff for dirty hands.
And brushes for under carpets.
And rods for netted curtains.
And spiders and darkness
and darkness and spiders.

And darkness

and darkness

and darkness.

He felt like the winters of childhood.
Ice on the inside
of the pane.

A GIRL, LIKE, Y'KNOW

When I met him, and that
I just liked him, and that
There was summat about him, y'know

And we was all a bit pissed, like
And we just sort of kissed, like
And ended up round the back, like, y'know

And then later, and that
When I found out and that
I was like, 'Fuckin' hell,' like, y'know

And I told him, and that
And I shown him, and that
And it just did his head in, y'know

And me Mam's like, 'No way,' like
But then she's ok, like
She's been dead good now, like, y'know

I'm like, 'Are you moving in, like?'
'To help with this kid, like?'
And he's like, 'Whatever,' y'know

So we got our own flat, like
But the area's crap, like
And we need *loads* of stuff, like, y'know

And then – I had Kyle, like
And now – for a while, like
I've felt a bit – shit, like, y'know

And he – hits me, and that
And he's – kicked me, and that
But – I – I – I love him, and that, like, you know?

And – sometimes – I feel, like
I've – ruined me life, like
But then I'm like – 'What life?' You know?

NOWHERE MAN

And sometimes she looks dead hard like, y'know
And sometimes she looks well fit
And sometimes she looks dead tired like, y'know
And sometimes she looks like shit

And sometimes she's all made up like, y'know
And sometimes she's straight from bed
And sometimes she's dead grown up like, y'know
And sometimes she's grown up dead

And sometimes she dun't say much like, y'know
And sometimes she takes a while
And sometimes it dun't take much like, y'know
And sometimes I think she smiles

And sometimes I think she likes me, y'know
And sometimes she just goes red
And sometimes I think about her, y'know
And sometimes I shoulda said

And sometimes she shoulda known like, y'know
And sometimes I think she does
And sometimes she's on her own like, y' know
And sometimes she looks at us

But sometimes I wanna tell her, y'know
And sometimes I think I should
But sometimes I wanna kill her, y'know
And sometimes I think I could

But sometimes she has the kid like, y'know
And sometimes he looks dead sad
And sometimes he looks dead big like, y'know
And sometimes just like his dad

And sometimes I think that – maybe, y'know
And sometimes I wanna try

And sometimes I think – the baby, y'know
And sometimes I wanna cry

And sometimes I just feel angry, y'know
And sometimes I just feel used
And sometimes I just feel empty, y'know
But most times I feel confused

And sometimes she's with her Mam like, y'know
And sometimes she's with her Nan
But she's never with her Dad like, y'know
She don't know where's The Nowhere Man?

She don't know where's The Nowhere Man?
She don't know where's The Nowhere Man?
Don't know where's the Nowhere Man?
Don't know where's The Nowhere Man?

...

Back turned to the wind;
the schoolboy without a coat
lights a cigarette.

Hunched on street corners.
Blank eyes hidden beneath caps.
Waiting. For a war.

'Things are looking up, kids!'
he said,
unveiling their first pot to piss in.

'Most people lead lives of quiet desperation and go to the grave with the song still in them.'
Henry David Thoreau

DRASTIC SURGERY

A cold Monday morning, a queue to the door
Breath steams up windows, coats drip on floors
Pushchairs and wheelchairs and zimmers and sticks
Bring the old and the cold and the poor and the sick

'He can't get it up.' 'She can't keep it down.'
'He keeps throwing up.' 'Is it meant to be brown?'
'I can't get to sleep.' 'I can't keep awake.'
There's heartache and heartbreak and shivers and shakes

The grandad whose hold on his bladder has lessened
The auntie depressed by her anti-depressants
The Tupperware beakers of strange coloured pee
The things wrapped in hankies that no man should see

The lush full of thrush then a rush of hot flushes
The drug pusher sick from the drug that he pushes
The mum of the druggie, her own drugs inside her
The children of drinkers who puke up on cider

The people made sick by a lifetime of labours
The people made ill by the lifestyle of neighbours
The kids missing school due to chronic sore throats
Walk from homes filled with smoke in inadequate coats

The 'work-shy malingerers' and 'chronic lead-swingers'
And those diagnosed by their stained yellow fingers
The sick notes for fit blokes, the big toes gone manky
The sex lives of ex-wives with no hanky-panky

The old man from Poland with Auschwitz tattoos
The self-preservation by pickling in booze
The overweight mum brings her overweight daughter
Breakfast consists of the Mars bar she bought her

13 and pregnant – 26 weeks
Too late to 'get rid of', the mother/child weeps
The parents and teachers, the neighbours, relations
Their judgement will scald her – 'Congratulations?'

And the drinkers come in for repeated prescriptions
'Same again, love?' No need for descriptions
And every day junkies with everyday tales
Of how yesterday's system every day fails

The young mum aged 30 is riddled with cancer
Her two simple questions get no simple answers
Desperation, frustration; anger, despair
Her kids facing Care Homes that don't *seem* to care

The ailments and ointments, constipation and boils
Conditions, emissions, inflammation and coils
The ulcers and pulses and dodgy auld tickers
The itching and scratching and delving in knickers

The anaemic, bulimic, anorexic, obese
Diabetics, epileptics, antiseptics and yeast
Diarrhoea, pyorrhoea, gonorrhoea and flu
Prescriptions, afflictions; ME, NSU

The bad breaths and cot deaths, the lotions and potions
The fevers and grievers, the going through the motions
The widows with shadows, the kids who can't play
The palavers with fathers now farther away

The verruca'd, the snookered, the dribble and drool
The crippled, cracked nipples and blood in the stools
Diagnosis, cirrhosis, prognosis, and piles
The lung cancer, young cancer, teardrops and smiles

The neck pain and back pain, the pains in the arse
The bathos and pathos, the drama and farce
Hepatitis, colitis and fungal infections
Tonsillitis, arthritis and jungle injections

The aches and the pains and the snot and the sneezes
The breaks and the sprains and the coughs and the wheezes
The toddlers teething and babies not feeding
The choking and heaving and trouble with breathing

The asthma and eczema, the piercings gone septic
The beer guts, the tear ducts, the chronic dyspeptics
The pimples and samples and things spat in jars
The kids hit by men driving family cars

The anxious, the stressed and the cold and the lonely
The clinically depressed and the old folks who only
Want *someone* to talk to, to save an hour's heating
The wife beater's wife and the latest wife beating

The infertile, the pregnant, the dazed and confused
The indignant malignant, the raped and abused
The weeping of women and children and sores
The unsettled stomachs and unsettled scores

The weight and the pressure, the strain and the shame
The grind on the mind of the names in the frame
The homebirths and stillbirths and kids stuck on glue
Failed marriage, miscarriage then beat black and blue

And sadness and madness and badness and spite
And moaning and groaning and grieving and *shite*
And vomit and grommets and fuss, puss and piss
And fist fights and last rites, and *no-one* to kiss

The old woman's life mapped in varicose veins
The young woman cutting to let out the pain
When years come too early, when help comes too late
When lives worse than death end in deaths worse than fate

But desperately cheerful, we'll say, 'Mustn't grumble.'
'You have to keep going.' 'There's worse off,' we mumble
And clutching prescriptions for tablets of stone
Post office, pharmacy, scratch-card and home

Who's next?

IT'S ALL GOING POSH DOWN THE PRECINCT

It's all going posh down the precinct.
The yuppies are coming to get yer!
Last week they closed down the Poundland
and opened a new EuroStretcher.

And they're ripping out all of the boozers
and opening them 'café bars.'
Where strangers avoid conversations
and no one can play you at darts.

And they don't serve mild or bitter!
Just lager and cocktails and vino.
And you can't get a brew like you used to,
just froth that they call 'Crappacino'.

And they want two pound ten for a cola!
When a litre is 29p!
So *someone's* extracting the urine!
But they won't be extracting from me!

And you can't get a good bacon butty,
just a 'BLT on ciabatta'.
With every known sauce except HP
and gallons of that fizzy watter.

And this girl gave me leaflets for sunbeds!
It was all I could do not to thump her!
I will die the colour God made me.
Not a cancerous, fried Umpalumpa!

And they opened a new public toilet
with a glittering civic occasion.
The Mayor didn't laugh when I asked him,
'Is Gents short for gentrification?'

Yes, it's all going posh down the precinct,
but I'm thinking of sending a letter.
If my life doesn't fit with this lifestyle,
how has it got any better?

NO MONEY

Three kids.

No money.

He drinks.

No money.

Four walls.

No money.

Fuck all.

No money.

No friends. No money.
Wits' end. No money.
Long queues. No money.
Bad news. No money.
Red bills. No money. Cheap thrills. No money.
No choice. No money. No voice. No money.
No say. No money. No way. No money.
No help. No money. No self. No money.
Get caught. No money. In court. No money.
No joke. No money. No hope. No money.
No money. No money. No money. No money. No money. No money.
NO MONEY!

NO WALLS

No walls.
But I am held
captive.

No ceiling.
But I am pressed
down.

No roof.
But I am covered
over.

No doors.
But I am locked
out.

No windows.
But I am still
broken.

No floor.
But I share your
earth.

DEBRIS

Club flyers dance
on the chill winds of morning.
Their tumbleweed promise of
good times, not seen.

Chip-sick lies frozen
with sun, shyly dawning
on ketchup lay bleeding
in vinegar steam.

> A footprint in dog-shit.
> Dead flowers on railings.
> And condom filled corners
> like sperm bank cashiers.

> Freeze frame reminders
> of perma-frost failings.
> Of half-lives, half-frozen
> with knee tremble tears.

Ice in shop doorways;
green crystal cascading
with stalactite piss-scapes
and rainbow displays.

Cold blood in needles;
re-pulsed on cracked paving.
'The future is orange'
each cap laughs and says.

> Alco Pop Stardom,
> just dregs left remaining.
> And face down in a cellar
> where sun never kissed.

Used and abandoned,
left shattered and draining.
The shell of a daughter;

not lost,

found

or missed.

SAVING DEPOSITS

With slut butter kisses on
fumble fuck mornings.

With floppy cock kisses and
yellow toothed smiles.

With best bitter kisses and
knuckle dust warnings.

She rubs for three wishes and
thousands of miles.

With smoker's cough kisses and
family infections.

With vindaloo kisses and
Dad's Day cologne.

With spunk drunkard kisses and
lethal injections.

She rubs for three wishes
and sends the cheques home.

NO MARK

Fences and walls,
bus stops and chip shops;
she would write her name
on to anything
that would listen.
Etched, never scrawled.

At 14, she carved half
her name into her arm with
the posh kid's pen.
'Incomplete. See me.'

At 19 she started.

Pricks in her arm, pricks in her mouth
Pricks in her arm, pricks in her mouth
Pricksinherarmpricksinhermouth
Pricksinherarmpricksinhermouth
Pricks in her life.

At 27
she *stopped.*

Just a
stain
in a car park, lined in chalk.

Just a
face
in the paper, peering through chips.

Not smiling on the local news.
The girl in the back row
looking down.

Circled.

And to think...

everyone always told her
that she would
never

leave a mark.

FOUND

All her life
she was lost.

Until one day
she was found

by an old man
walking his dog.

TINY DREAMS

Conceived against a shit-house wall,
she was born against the odds.
But then the pastors and her masters
called her bastard before God.

And they told her she was *nothing*.
And nothing's all she knew.
So she fought and schemed her tiny dreams
'cos tiny dreams come true.

Dreams of liberty and dignity,
to know love and respect;
in place of loneliness and poverty
and cruelty and neglect.

And she found her local library
was a flawed but loyal friend.
With its once upon a time for bed,
live happily, the end.

And she found those books of public schools
with wheezes, japes and schemes,
just domestic science fiction,
so she kept her tiny dreams.

Then she thought she'd found a good lad,
who wouldn't hit her. Much.
But he kept her full of children,
then he wouldn't keep in touch.

And so what's a girl supposed to do
when she's never known true love?
From a mother's hand or lover man
or brother man above.

She just does her best, like all the rest,
to keep the wolves away,

until the Welfare states the welfare
of her children's pulled away.

And she's left back on her own again,
but... *emptier* than before.
Just forgotten rotten apple,
peeled and bitten to the core.

And she fights to win them back again,
but loses every round.
Until her sanity, humanity
and tiny dreams are drowned.

Now she lives on fags and bad news,
washed down with cheap regrets
of her own if-only loneliness.
Forgive-me-not forgets.

And she sleeps on eider-downsides
under poly-festered covers
that smell of cheap cologne-liness
and the promises of others.

And she wakes up to a bad dream
and stales in bed all day.
Like a sad ghost with a bad dose
of hound-dog groundhog day.

But she doesn't hate the father,
they were sixteen, seventeen.
And he dared to show her kindness,
but was scared by tiny dreams.

And for one time in her life back then
she believed she had some worth:
as a lover, as a mother,
as a citizen of Earth.

Still she finds her local library
is welcoming and warm.
She finds comfort there and summat there
that makes her feel reborn.

And she scours through the pages
for that rarest thing in art,
truth and beauty in the rages
of a kindred spirit heart.

And she finds few words that touch a nerve,
one for every mile of shelf.
So she hides away and scribes away
and writes the book herself.

And she bleeds it in a notebook
with a pen held like a knife
to the hacking throat of fortune
in the death throes of a life.

And she tears it from her writing pad
and *hides it in a drawer.*
But if you think about the life she's had
and what she's writing for:

it's her tiny dreams of dignity;
to know love and respect,
in place of loneliness and poverty
and cruelty and neglect.

And you'll find only one conclusion,
find the one important sign.
There'll be beauty, truth and poetry
in every fucking line.

SOMEONE

And she made do wi' *nowt.*
And she never said owt.
But she shoulda said summat to someone.

If you haven't got owt.
You can never say owt.
And she never got no help from no-one.

But *I'll* tell you summat.
And I'll tell you for nowt.
See, she never did no harm to no-one.

And she'd do owt for nowt.
And she'd never tek owt.
And that's summat

should make you
a someone.

GOING NOWHERE

The lights change.

But you're going nowhere.

So you sit there

thinking

about your shit car and
your shit job and
your shit boss and
your shit marriage and
your shit choices and
your tight waistband and
your wild kids and
your red bills and
your father's death and
your mother's pain
and

That.

New.

Lump.

The lights change.

But you're going nowhere.

He saw two magpies,
but experienced no joy; just
double sorrow.

HO! HO! HO!

The child in the photo has a gap-toothed smile,
    glitterball eyes, dancing with promise,
    beautiful but shy
    like tinsel
    fresh from the box.

    The old man is 'smiling' too.
    New teeth,
    bared,
    beneath a cheap, white beard.

    All false.

    His sad eyes,
    red on white, quietly pleading,
    'God, give me strength.'

    ~

Creased and faded now,
    the child seldom smiles,
    but aches and moans
    and pains and groans
    from Christmas to Christmas
    to Christmas.

    The old man?
    Died.
    Alone.

    But the Ghosts of Christmas Past,
    forever and ever,
    and ever, and ever,
    and ever, and ever,
    and ever,

    say, 'Cheese'.

'In the end it took me a dictionary to find out the
meaning of unrequited.'
Billy Bragg, The Saturday Boy

She pulled petals from daisies
and thought that he loved her.

He loved her not.

LOVER'S LAMENT

I bought her flowers

from Esso.

Designer clothes

from Tesco.

Fine champagne

from Netto.

She said, 'No.'

SPANGLES

She had this *filthy* giggle!
And a captivating wiggle.
And a sexy little jiggle as she walked.

And her arms were charmed with bangles
and they'd jingle and they'd jangle
and they'd sparkle and they'd spangle as she talked.

      Like the stardust that was sprinkled
      in her eyes to make them twinkle.
      And the cutest little wrinkle when she smiled.

      And she had this graceful waddle
      that would grace a supermodel.
      When she walked me home – it nearly drove me wild!

So, one night, I softly nudged her
and I told her that I loved her.
But I guess that I misjudged her 'cos she laughed.

And she jangled and she jiggled.
And she spangled and she wiggled
And she wriggled as she giggled, 'Don't be daft!'

      Then, despite all my insistence,
      my delusional persistence,
      she began to keep her distance, I would find.

      And so, much to my confusion,
      I came round to the conclusion
      that our love was an illusion in my mind.

And *it's not* her filthy giggle.
Or her captivating wiggle.
Or the sexy little jiggle of her thighs.

I miss the music from her bangles.
And her jingles and her jangles.
And the sparkles and the spangles in her eyes.

BATTERED

In *my life* her batter's the one thing that matters.
Her tabard, her hairnet, her lippy!
Can I takeaway kisses? Maybe make her my missus?
I love how she smells – like a Chippy!

I love how her eyes light up blue as the flies
get bedazzled and (bzzz) frazzled to nothing.
I go weak at the knees at the sensual ease
with which sausages slip into muffins.

I'm loopy and dazed as she scoops into trays
dripping juices all over me portions.
I melt as she bends to the fridge at the end
I can say 'chicken breast' but with caution.

Oh, to lie in her arms! Slip my fries in her barms!
High on mushies – the drug that she pushes.
She's so pert I'm half-crazed as she squirts mayonnaise.
(Do you think I've got one of me crushes?)

Should I whisper, 'Your eyes look like two Holland's pies?'
Kiss her cruet, say, 'Baby, let's do it?'
Tell her, 'Baby, your lips taste like gravy and chips.
And your breasts are like puddings of suet?'

She works on me scallops, spurts me ketchup in dollops
as I ask, 'Any chance of a ffff-fork?'
I didn't piss on me chips, but no kiss on the lips,
she just gave me a pet name – 'sad dork'.

So last night at eleven with sights set on heaven,
I told her I loved her, when plastered.
It plunged into havoc, she lunged with a haddock
and, *'Piss off you fat, greasy bastard!'*

WWW.WALNUTWHIPPED.CO.UK

She looked for men in pick 'n' mix,
And hooked them when she licked their Twix.
She poked inside my pacamac
and stroked behind my knacker sac.

As we repaired to a hotel room
I was not prepared for a total loon
who'd hush my lips with gaffa tape,
and brush my nips with Jaffa Cakes.

She fixed me down with liquorice laces,
licked around my ticklish places.
My chest was oiled with urine. Piss!
(My vest was spoiled during this.)

I said, 'Jesus! You're a total nutter!'
She greased us up with cocoa butter
and stuffed my arse with M&Ms,
a Fudge, a Mars and Midget Gems.

She dressed up as a big fat monkey.
Stressed us with a Kit-Kat Chunky,
the Spotted Dick inside her knickers,
a Topic, a Twix and a deep-fried Snickers.

She clipped off all my short and curlies,
whipped my balls with Curly-Wurlies.
She went a little crazy next.
She knelt and we had (sniff) nasal sex.

And then I spied her mate, you know,
he was hiding tapes and videos.
And now my shame is viewed on line.
My name is Googled all the time.

It takes a million hits a day.
They'll make a billion quid that way.
But my ring still gives a constant crunch
from the things she did with Monster Munch.

'Love is all.'
Jack Kerouac

SOMEONE WARM TO HOLD

(From Love v Lust team slam tour, Commonword, 2007)

There's chocolate bars and dodgem cars
And falling leaves and record sleeves
And writing rhymes and 99s
I quite like all of those

And loud guitars and edgy bars
And taking baths and photographs
And starry nights and tickle fights
Are favourites, I suppose

And rocky shores and windswept moors
And climbing hills of daffodils
And flying kites and riding bikes
Can sometimes leave me cold

> But the greatest thing in all the world
> The greatest thing in all the world
> The greatest thing in *all the world*
> Is someone warm to hold

And candyfloss and lollipops
And buttered toast and Sunday roasts
And 'tater 'ash and piles of mash
Will always get my vote

And fish and chips and skinnydips
And Holland's pies and butterflies
And setting suns and bubbleguns
Can often float my boat

But MP3s and DVDs?
And flashy cars and push-up bras?
And camera phones? Designer homes?
Are 'must-haves', so we're told!

But the greatest thing in all the world
The greatest thing in all the world
The greatest thing in all the world
Is someone warm to hold

Now we're all dealt cards of love and lust
So play your lust cards if you must
But me? I'll stick not twist and bust
Snap! We'll never fold

But look into their lustful eyes
Through the windows, through the lies
They'd swap it *all* and more besides
For someone warm to hold

So play the field if that's your thing
And skip and swing and everything
But watch for slides that go with swings
That's something *they've* not told

But someone's got to dish the dirt
Contact sports? Someone gets hurt!
For me the game that's always worked
Is someone warm to hold

Find some *one* to share your lives
Keep love, and lust, awake, alive
Nurture them for all your lives
To grow as you grow old

      Because the greatest thing in all the world
      The *greatest thing* in all the world
      The *greatest thing in all the world*
      Is someone warm to hold

INTIMACY

I slip into bed and
pour myself around her.
Over, under, behind.
Inside.

My knees jigsaw into
the hollows behind hers.
I hug her contours like marzipan.
I get *under* her perfume.

My cock stirs and nestles blissfully
between her cheeks
as I run my hand
up her thigh,
over her hips
around her waist and
slide it under her breasts.
Heavy on my fingers.
Warm against my arm.

Our insteps dovetail
like yin and yang,
as I kiss her neck
through scented hair.

She smiles in her sleep,
and snuggles back towards me.

I squeeze her tenderly
and she softly,

gently,

farts.

I CAN WRITE A RAINBOW

Red and yellow and pink and green;
orange and purple and blue.

I can write a rainbow.
I can write a rainbow.
I can write a rainbow
for you.

I've got a new word for 'thesaurus!'

I'm inventing a whole new language;
finding new vowel sounds,
exploring lost consonants.
Not just re-writing the dictionary,
but renaming it, baby!

I'm articulating the unsaid,
naming the unspoken;
drafting and crafting more volumes
than I have yet developed numbers

I'm making up new words.
Dreaming up an entire lexicon.
Delightful and insightful,
musical and beautiful.
Poly-decametrical
and symbio-symetrical.
Gentle on the eardrums
like the sneeze of baby angels.

I'm re-defining emotions.
Categorising and sub-categorising
a thousand thousand types of joy
and a million billion beauties.
Switching subtleties and nuances
for kiss, kiss, kiss, kiss, kisses.

They say that the human eye
can distinguish more than sixteen million colours.
I'll name them *all*, if I'm to write a rainbow for you.

And for this new language?
I have a whole new alphabet.
Twenty thousand hieroglyphs of such exquisite beauty
that I need new words to even *begin* to describe them.
A font so intricate and delicate
that the reader may be forgiven for sobbing
even before they are assembled into words.

But assemble them I must.
I'm writing spells and incantations,
and prayers and hymns and gospels
of poetry *so holy* that the very gods will weep.

But only when I've found a name for the *sound* of dew on roses.
And only when I've made the word for the *kiss* of cream on peaches.
And only when I've named the shades of *all* of God's creation.

Then and only then.
Then and only then.
Then and *only then*

can I say
how much
I love you.

In red and yellow and pink and green
and orange and purple and blue
and *sixteen million colours!*
I can write a rainbow!
I *can* write a rainbow!
I can write a rainbow

for *you*.

BOHEMIAN RASPBERRY

And your love is like a fairy cake
And it's soft and sweet and fills me
And your love is like a fairground ride
And it never stops to thrill me

And your love is like an ice-cream
And I'm the ripple in your raspberry
And your love is so Bohemian
That you've got me in a rhapsody

And your love is like the warmest lake
And I want to swim and drown there
And your love is like that perfect place
And I want to settle down there

And your love is like a railroad train
And I want to be your hobo
And your love is irie, superfly
And I want to win your MOBO

And your love is like Las Vegas
And I want to be your Elvis
And your love is Rock-A-Hula, baby
Let me be your pelvis

And your love is like a magnet
And I'm totally attracted
And your love is like a takeaway
And I want to be subtracted

And your love is like a dialect
And I want to be your patois
And your love is like a holy war
And I want to be your fatwa

And your love is like a pantomime
And I'm your slapstick violence
And your love is a cathedral
And I want to be your (silence)

And your love is like a rocket ship
And I want to be your astronaut
And your love is like a shopping trip
And I want to be the shit you bought

And your love is like a road trip
And I want to hit the highway
And your love is like Sinatra
And I want to be your My Way

And your love is like Franz Schubert
And I finish off your symphony
And your love is like a tragedy
And I'm your tea and sympathy

And your love is like a forest fire
And I want you to consume me
And your love is like a grave-robber
And I want you to exhume me

And your love is like a Chinese film
And I'm the Flying Daggers
And your love is like a lover's lips
And baby, I'm Mick Jagger's

And your love is like a puzzled face
And I want to make it quizzical
And your love is like that song and
'Let's get physical, physical'

And your love is like a laughter line
And I want to be your wrinkle
And your love is like a garden
And I want to be your sprinkle

And your love is like a Phd
And I could be your thesis
And your love is like a jigsaw
Baby, I'm the missing pieces

And your love is like a Carry On film
I'm your innuendo
And your love is like *when angels sing*
And I'm the last crescendo

And your love is like Da Vinci
Baby, I'm your Mona Lisa
And your love is like an Arctic scene
And I'm your red hot geyser

And your love is like a miracle
And God, I'm loaves and fishes
And your love is like Aladdin's lamp
And you'd be all three wishes

And your love is like religion
And I want to come together
And your love is like infinity
And I want

to be

forever

THREE WISHES

They can feed me with rust,
They can slice me with jewels,
They can nail me to verdigris statues of slaves.
They can grind me to dust,
They can chain me to fools,
They can burn me to cinders and dance on my grave.

You can *heal* my twig bones,
You can stitch me with kisses,
You can ease me from crosses and spice me like Christ.
You can roll away stones,
You can grant me three wishes,
You can love me, and hold me for all of my life.

LET'S MAKE A LOVE

Now the audience knows in the corniest poems
that *'together'* and *'forever'* will rhyme.
And something about *'hearts,'* gushing *'we'll never part'*
'til forever!' Whatever! *'...all time.'*

And a naff line with *'lady.'* A half rhyme with *'crazy.'*
And maybe a *'baby!'* or two.
So I guess it's too simple to confess to goose pimples
when I think about thinking of you.

> But I don't care!

> So let's make a life, girl! Let's make a love!
> Let's make a future together.
> Let's make a home, girl. Never alone, girl.
> Let's make a family together!

And we're right to be certain that we'll fight over curtains,
but you'll get your own way *so it ends!*
We'll have games and be silly. You'll give names to my willy,
just to text to your eight closest friends.

And we can shop 'til it aches, stop for coffees and cakes,
buying flowers and suitable rugs.
Oh, and roasters and toasters and posters and coasters.
And showers. And beautiful jugs.

Being daft and outrageous. See, laughter's contagious.
We'll smile as we file through the markets.
Buying trowels and clocks, trying towels and woks,
and fab-style, shag pile carpets.

So don't fret – there'll be sex, girl! Oh, yes, there'll be sex!
And not only with fingers and tongues.
There'll be fabulous, furious, feverish fffforeplay.
Then slowly. And holy. And long.

And we'll plaster me nipples with raspberry ripples.
Get slippery, slithery, slinky.
We'll use gallons of lube, need huge flagons not tubes
as we put the KY into kinky!

And there'll be gentleness, giggles and tenderness, tickles,
make snowmen and roam in the park.
There'll be movies and smoothies, a few boogie-woogies
and smoochies at home in the dark.

There'll be rubs when you're aching and hugs when you're shaking.
I'll shoulder your cares when you're sleeping.
There'll be huddles and cuddles, and huggles and snuggles.
I'll stroke at you hair when you're sleeping.

And we may not have riches, but who says what rich is?
Bare lists of belongings and things?
No. I'm telling you this, at a penny kiss
We'll share *riches beyond those of kings!*

> So *let's* make a life, girl! *Let's* make a love!
> Let's make a future together.
> Let's make a home, girl. Never alone, girl.
> Let's make a family together!

And maybe I'm crazy, but may I say lady,
hey, let's make a baby or two!
Cos I'm certain your beauty is worth reproducing.
I want to make babies with you.

So, yes, there'll be children. *If* we're blessed to be with them.
Our love as a girl and a boy.
As the manifestation of our mad adoration.
Our love as a girl and a boy.

And there'll be teething and crawling, and feeding and bawling,
and smiling, and nice times, and pleasures.

And glitter and glue sticks, and kittens and Pooh sticks;
compiling a lifetime of treasures.

And when we're old and we're lumpy,
when roads appear bumpy,
when autumn leaves chills on our days.
Well, we'll face it together. We'll embrace it together.
Be *awesome*, be silver not grey.

And we'll have Breakfast at Tiffany's. Sexual epiphanies.
Fornicate, foxtrot and feast.
Staying so very active, no way geriatric.
Not sprightly, twice nightly at least!

And we'll *dance on the table* each chance that we're able.
This love grows, it doesn't grow weaker.
With our days getting numbered, I'm amazed and yet humbled.
It's deeper. And deeper. And deeper.

And still *so* fundamental we *will not* go gentle
into that good night without a good fight.
We will *not* act our age, we will *blaze* against beige.
We will *rage* into the dying of the light.

Until we're riddled with cancers.
With… riddles for answers.
Together. When push comes to shove.
We must… share the same gravestone.
Just the… pair of our names shown.
Forever. When hush comes to love.

'Making the decision to have a child – it is momentous. It is to decide forever to have your heart go walking around outside your body.'
Elizabeth Stone

Baby smiling in
a supermarket trolley.
Not for sale. Sadly.

NOTHING NEW

She walks down the aisle.

     Music plays.

     She's not late.

     She doesn't smile.

     She gives herself away.

She walks down the aisle.

     No flowers or bridegroom.

     No family or friends.

     No chauffeurs to show for.

     No singing but prayers.

She walks down the aisle.

     Nothing old – but ticking.

     Nothing new – if only.

     Nothing borrowed – but envied.

     Nothing blue. That's covered.

She walks down the aisle.

     Nappies and wipes and

     soothers and buds and

     potions and formulas.

     Magic and miracles.

She walks down the aisle.

> Women and babies and
>
> young girls and babies and
>
> children and babies and
>
> babies and babies and...

She walks down the aisle.

> Tissues and chocolate and
>
> red wine and cat food and
>
> flowers for her sister and
>
> tampons and pads.

CAKE HOLE

For Joseph

Tears.
Ready salted tears.
And his perfect little cake hole
so contorted as to reveal
the jagged morning tooth-scape
to the never-changing dawn.

The gaps – all filled with pride.
The 'Will-They-Won't-Theys.'
The 'What's Up Docs?'
And those nearly nine years old.

Painful yet exciting,
like all rites of passage.
An hourly, daily, weekly, monthly, yearly
shifting toothscape.
An epic traced by tongue and mirror and
re-re-re-reminded with every single brush stroke
and every morsel chewed
'Da-ad! Yeah, right! Like I can eat an apple! *Derrr!*'

A big deal
for a little big boy.
His pyjamas looking smaller now,
than just the other day.

(Sings) 'All I want for Christmas is me two front teeth'
'Me two front…'
'Daaaad!'

'She's not been!'
'*She's not been!*' he cries
to a mother, she is risen
and a father's cursing corpse.
Each re-re-re-remembering
that they've forgotten to remember.

87

'You're up too early!'
'We told you last time.'
'Go back to bed.'
'Give her a chance.'

'Yeah, right!'
'You and Mum take 'em and leave a pound.
I knew it all along! *I told you!'*
'I bet you just chuck 'em away, don't you?'
Spat as snot in bitter bubbles
wiped from lip to 'jama sleeve
Dr Ninja Thingy Wotsit Wotsit watching.

'*Shhh!* You'll wake your sister!'
As he sobs into bed with his Dad, and Mum pounds
her way to his bedroom to cushion the blow.

Pocketing her trophy to be velveted like jewels.

'*Look!* Come here! You've missed it.
There! You Charlie!'

'Yeah, right!' he says.

But his perfect little cake hole is happy now.
Gurning out a silly smile.
Sugar coated, family sized.

So contorted as to reveal
the latest little hole in

his innocence.

HAPPY MEALS

Hiya.

I'll have a white, stodgy bread roll please –
made from bleached white flour.
High in salt, low in nutrients,
smeared in high fat spreads.
Lots of salty, sugary ketchup please.
Butter, yeah, mayonnaise, yeah.
And onion rings. Yep, cheers.

Hold the lettuce.

And an artery clogging burger please –
made from genetically modified
mechanically reclaimed meat slurry –
faces, feet, arseholes, fat,
rusk, fat, water, salt, fat, artificial flavourings, artificial colourings,
sodium.
And E 174, 295, 473 and 893…
286, 699 and 304.

And fat.

From cows fed on other cows
and marinated in anti-biotics, anti-oxidants, growth hormones,
pesticides, stabilisers, dextrose and sodium metabisulphite.

Erm, extra large fries please.

And a Diet Coke.

Yeah, large.

Cheers.

There you go.

Say 'thank you' to the nice man.

Dad was World Farting Champion.
No-one
could hold a candle to him.

He was philosophical
about his constipation.

Shit happens.

SMALL ELEPHANTS

The father taught his son a line,
remembered from his own childhood,
on how to spell 'because.'

'Big Elephants Can Always Understand Small Elephants,' he said.

The boy laughed,
and his father smiled.

Because

he understood

that the child would

never

forget.

STUCK AT THE LIGHTS

Flowers on a railing
with a favourite teddy bear.
Fixed with love and Sellotape
for the childhood taken there.

Cars are stopped then speed away
but signal how they feel.
Some will cast a fleeting glance,
some cast out Happy Meals.

Grandma tidies twice a day,
takes cans and Styrofoam,
but the mother, like the driver,
always takes the long way home.

'Accident Here' sign. 'Can U Help?'
Ignored, obscured by dirt.
Let's print the sign on Grandma's hat
and the breast of Mummy's shirt.

The strong man struggles
to bear
the tiny coffin.

MOTHER'S DAY

Levels of suicide and self-harm amongst women prisoners in England and Wales are at a record high. BMJ.com (2004). Levels peak around Mother's Day.
Eric Allison, Prison Correspondent, The Guardian

A pain. That wakes me. Every day.
Waving – as they walk away.
Things I always meant to say
with love on Mother's Day.

Body clock alarm bells sound.
'Sorry, Mam – I've let you down.'
Kids cry – and I'm not around
with love on Mother's Day.

The card awaited – doesn't come.
Late – addressed to 'World's Best Mum'.
Tears – make homemade colours run
with love on Mother's Day.

The baby who – I've never seen.
Forms I signed aged seventeen.
Tortured by what could have been
with love on Mother's Day

The man who left – without a care.
The scan that said – there's nothing there.
The chance to comb a daughter's hair
with love on Mother's Day.

The mother who – I never knew.
Nursery empty – painted blue.
Where the fuckin' hell were you
with *'love'* on Mother's Day?

Mother Nature's cruellest curse.
Photos fading in a purse.
Cut myself before I

Cut myself before I
Cut myself before I *burst*
with love on Mother's Day.

The hardest thing I *ever* wrote.
'*Please*. Forgive me,' quote/unquote.
Kiss, kiss, kiss to end the note.
With love – on Mother's Day.

Flowers spell her name.
Angela. Angela. Ange.

One set just says: MAM.

'The course of true love never did run smooth.'
William Shakespeare

They smiled. They kissed. They fucked.
He left.

She caught his disease.

But not his name.

SHE NEVER

Now I think about it...

She never had her roots showing
She never had a hair out of place

She never left the house without make up
She never answered the door in her dressing gown

She never left the pots unwashed
She never ate from the pan

She never left the bed unmade
She never let the bills go red

She never forgot to flush
She never left the top off the toothpaste

She never let her underwear turn grey
She never sniffed and wore it anyway

She never *talked* about a baby – but...
She never *thought* about anything else and

She never went to christenings and
She never coo-ed at children and

She never said she loved me but
She never said she didn't and

She never ever faked it but
She never ever had one and

She never ever smiled at me
She never ever smiled and

She never said she loved me

But she never

Ever

FLAMMABLE

'Flammable'
and 'inflammable.'

Sometimes words and phrases
which appear to be opposites
can, in fact, share the same meaning.

Like, 'I love you,' and
'Fuck off and die!'

KEPT IN THE DARK

He turned off the light so
he
could see,
not his wife
but his sexual fantasy.

He turned on the light when
he
was done.
His wife, was still there, and the

rough boys had gone.

He never guessed that she knew.
But then, she knew
that he would never guess.

NOT KNOWING

Every night,
he sat
and cried and
wrote
his secret poems.

He never spoke

a single word.

He didn't want

her

knowing.

Every day,
she'd sit
and cry and
read
his secret poems.

She *couldn't breathe*

a single word.

She didn't *want him,*

knowing.

SOMETIMES

And sometimes

On warm summer nights and the frostiest mornings
And sometimes

On those Hate The World days that arrive without warnings
And sometimes

I wake up alone to a desolate aching
And sometimes

I see my reflection all cracking and breaking
And sometimes

When letters arrive to a Mr and Mrs
And sometimes

When Christmas is Christmas with no Christmas kisses
And sometimes

When I'm eating it cold from a tin in the kitchen
And sometimes

When I'm stood in the line to collect my prescription
And sometimes

In all my hours sleeping and most of them waking
And sometimes

I shake when I drink and I drink 'cos I'm shaking
And sometimes

When people we knew nudge and then look right through me
And sometimes

When I think what I started and what it's done *to* me
And sometimes

When Mam became Grandma and, *Christ*, how it thrilled her
And sometimes

When she told me she knew then how quickly it killed her
And sometimes

When I think of you telling our children my failings
And sometimes

When I stand outside school and just *cling* to the railings
And sometimes

When I'm locked in the toilet in shops and – just *bawling*
And sometimes

When dialling your number to hear the recording
And sometimes

When seeing your face in the face of our baby
And sometimes

When seeing *my* face in the face of our baby
And sometimes

When seeing *me Mam* in the face of our baby
And sometimes

When seeing *That Man* kiss the face of our baby
And sometimes

And sometimes

And sometimes

The sun
on my daughter;

beaming.

PHISH OUT OF WATER

Always surfing online
Through a cesspit of whine
Bleeding need for the sharks there to bite him
Caught in web-nets once more
Flaps for breath on the floor
Always phishing for strangers to 'like' him

And he wanders round chatrooms
And squanders in twat rooms
Bone lonely in virtual crowds
And he wanks himself dry
When he LOLs – it's a lie
But there's *nothing* – for Crying Out Loud

And he'll browse around porn sites
Un-aroused by the porn shite
Spunks issues on tissues and mags
And he eats finger lickin'
Feels choked like a chicken
'Til he gets KFC-sick and gags

And he rubs for three wishes
But forgets what his wish is
More cum numb with each pissing drink
He forgets to remember
Wet dreams left dismembered
And crackpots piled up in his sink

And he ought to forgive her
For the daughter now with her
But there's salt in his wounds and his scars
But, still frozen online
A tsunami each time
Their photo. He rates it.

Two stars.

The names tattooed through
the hearts on each arm were blacked
out; but not erased.

TATTOOED TIGERS

And he smelt like tattooed tigers
And he kissed like Christmas Day
And he felt like prayers answered
But he touched and ran away

And he held her like a lifebuoy
And he looked like Wedding Day
And he saw that she was floating
But he touched and ran away

And she gave birth to his baby
And she felt like New Year's Day
And she carried her. Then buried her.
But he touched and ran away

And she heard he'd found another
And she felt like Judgement Day
And she'd tasted death

and angel's breath

But he touched

and ran away

DON'T WASTE YOUR BREATH

Their love was all festooned
    With 'I Love You' balloons
        Their love was meant to last
            And filled with laughing gas

        Their love could not be stopped
            Until one day... it popped
                Their love danced all around
                    But slowly it went down

Their love... just died a death
    Like so much wasted breath
        Their love *was everything*
            But they let go of the string

        Their love *was* all festooned
            With 'I Love You' balloons
                Their love *was meant* to last
                    And filled with laughing gas

Their love was *everything*
    But they let go of the string
        Their love was bright. And gay.
        But then it blew away

        If *your* love's meant to last
            Keep it filled with laughing gas
        If *your* love's everything
        Always jump and

                catch the string

'Old age is the most unexpected of all things
that can happen to a man.'
Leon Trotsky

BOP 'TIL YOU DROP

(Tonight I'm Gonna Party Like I'm Nearly 99)
(Last Night A DJ Shaved My Wife)

If I boogie on down, I can't boogie back up
If I back flip, me back clicks and I'm totally stuffed
It's not much fun moshing if your bunions keep squashing
And I stopped body-popping 'cos me shoulder kept locking

Don't ask me to go-go 'cos that's just a no-no
I'm finding the pogo's becoming a no-go
I can't get satisfaction or go for the big notes
I wind up in traction with shed loads of sick notes

I sit out the smoochies, I can't hoochie coochie
I'm more cardy and slippers than Prada and Gucci
When it gets to the weekend I'm more Tesco than disco
'Cos me neck's badly weakened and I find that me hips go

I used to bop 'til I dropped
I used to rock round the clock
I used to hop to the pop 'til the beat don't stop
I need hip hop, hip hop, hip hop, hip hop, hip hop, hip hop, hip
operation

SMOKE LONELY

She knew she'd miss his hollow, in the sofa where they sat
And his rattle. And his whistle, tap and hum
But she never thought she'd miss the way he'd fart and blame the cat
Or his love poem, to Carol Vorderman's bum
She knew that she would miss him fixing everything, well nearly
And his blazing, scathing raving at the box
But she never thought she'd miss the way his eyes would speak so
clearly
Or his big toe, peeping through those *bloody socks*

She knew that she would miss the solid warmth of him in bed
And the bonds and vows and promises they shared
But she never thought she'd miss the way a map or A-Z
Would always lead to World War Three declared
She knew that she would miss the mirrored hearts he drew in steam
And the way they seemed to ghost back, every day
But she never thought she'd miss the crumbs of Death By Custard
Cream
Or the duvet's smooth manoeuvring his way

She knew she'd miss his prickled kiss; the man before he'd shaved
Re-born as baby-soft, and smooth, and clean
But she never thought she'd miss the woe betide mark when he
bathed
Or his fairy tales of princesses and queens
She knew she'd miss the way that he would hold her 'til first light
'I know,' he'd say. 'I know, I know, I know.'
But she never thought she'd miss him smoking lonely in the night
In the spare room with their heirlooms, kept just so

She knew she'd miss the way they'd cook for two - on Christmas Day
Their hopes afloat in toasts of blood red booze
But she never thought she'd miss his soft *Amen* when they would
pray
With their eyes closed tight to hide their baby blues
She knew she'd miss her young man, always strong and free and wild
How he'd take her, her expectant girlish screams

But she never thought she'd miss him, as an old man, like a child
Who'd mistake her

for the daughter

of their dreams

After the funeral she ate alone and
cooked for one

too many.

He keeps her grave well stocked with
fresh lilies.

She *fucking hated* lilies.

Confetti on gravestones
is silent but
resonates deeply.

CHERRY BLOSSOM

I brush off the mud and
wipe off the dust and
dry them.

Thoroughly.

Lovingly, even.

Just like you'd show me.

As my shoes grew ever bigger

than yours.

I take a blackened cloth and
spit on the toes and
shine them.

Patiently.

Lovingly, even.

Just like you'd show me.

Until the face I see reflected

is yours.

I rub until
I summon up
the genie
of your approval.

I wish
I wish

I wish it

wasn't muddy
by your grave.

ALWAYS THERE

And he loved the flesh and bones of him
The re-assuring tones of him
The never on your own of him
And he was always there

And he loved the very soul of him
The pieces and the whole of him
And every crease and hole of him
And he was always there

And he loved to kiss the face of him
To touch the special place of him
To orbit in the space of him
And he was always there

And he loved to feel the heat of him
To synchronize the beat of him
He worshipped at the feet of him
And he was *always there*

      And so when... the illness came for him
      When *nothing* was the same for him
      Just suffering and blame for him
      He was *always* there

      All through the longest nights for him
      The fevers and the fights for him
      The shivers and the shites for him
      He was always there

      Even though he often turned on him
      Got *nothing* in return from him
      But spit and spite and spurn from him
      He was *always there*

      Even when he had to bathe for him
      Shift his shit and shave for him

Cradle to the grave for him
He was *always there*

And so when... he missed the beat of him
Just... ashes from the heat of him
He knelt and kissed the feet of him
'Cos he was always there

And he bathed the earthly skin of him
Washed away the sin of him
The little boy within of him
And *he* was always there

And he loved the flesh and bones of him
The re-assuring tones of him
The never on your own of him
And he was always there

And though God... was never there for him
He says a favourite prayer for him
And saves a sacred chair for him
And he is... *always* there

She lived her life in
shrouded gloom. They found her dead
in the living room.

HOLLOW

After you'd gone

I saved your favourite cushion.

Setting it gently to one side,
lovingly
and full of care,
so as not to lose the shape of you.

Your lasting impression,
as it were.

Sometimes

I place my hand there
for comfort.

Often

I place my face there.
Gasping
for the smell of you.

And tracing
where your lipstick
left its mark.

I loved, I love, *I'll live* for you.
Like the promise
that you pressed from me.

~

I smother your memory.
A kismet of kisses.

And weep 'til I drown
your forgiveness.

LIFE GOES ON (For Mum, Elaine)

In land and seas
In birds and bees
In worlds
and worlds between them

In sand and brine
In space and time
In stars
and all who've seen them

In sun and silk
In mothers' milk
In fruits
and all who taste them

In trees and flowers
In years and hours
In days
and all who waste them

In soil and seeds
In words and deeds
In lights
and all who beam them

In smiles and tears
In hopes and fears
In dreams
and all who dream them

In rock and stone
In skin and bone
In ashes
and the small things

In breeze and breath
In life and death
In truth
I *am* in *all* things

Early snow falls
on my
late mother.

SCROLLING

Found between
forgotten friends

I've not scrolled through M
for a lifetime

> It was me who'd bought it for her,
> I remembered
>
> A happy birthday
>
> The numbers – not that big, really
>
> Phones 4 U, I recalled

We could unwrap it together then, joking

And I'd bowed to prize a kiss

She never used it, of course
She wasn't mobile herself

Unable to press the buttons
even when she could have seen them

Her voice – not always there

Her words – often missed

> For a moment though?
> We're re-connected!

'Hello? Hiya, love! *Fine!'*

Young again, we are

It's good to talk

In truth, I text
'I love u'

(How *do you do* those smiley faces,
lay on one side?)

    'Message could not be sent'
    I know

But today is not the day

that I'll delete Mum

from my phone

'Music? It's the noise that makes life bearable.'
Unknown

SPECIAL PLACE

Loneliness
Hopelessness
Helplessness
Emptiness

She sets fire to hope and sucks it in through a cigarette
Without a light from a friend, she takes the smouldering end
And lights another cigarette
She's not poor because she's smoking
She's smoking *because* she's poor
And it's the only thing warm in her life
And the only thing she's left to hold, apart from

Loneliness
Hopelessness
Helplessness
Emptiness

She takes a bottle of hope and drains a glass like she's needing it
She does the same thing again, and then again and again
Because – she's needing it
She's not lonely because she's drinking
She's drinking 'cos she's all alone
And it used to make her feel so alive
Now she needs it to ease the pain of

Loneliness
Hopelessness
Helplessness
Emptiness

She takes hope from its sleeve and puts the needle in the record's vein
She plays the same song again, and then again and again
Because he sings he loves a girl with her name
She's not smiling because she's dancing
She's dancing just to raise a smile
Because she never goes nowhere
And music can take her to a special place

Because she never goes nowhere
And music can take her to a special place

Because she never goes nowhere
And music can take her to that special place

Away from
Loneliness
Hopelessness
Helplessness
Emptiness

ROCK&ROLL

Brothers and Sisters!

Do *you* believe in Rock&Roll?
Say, 'I believe!'

Say, 'I believe!'

Yeah, I believe that Rock&Roll
can blow the mind and free the soul.
Can cultural revolutionise
and change a generation's lives.

Because...
my life was saved aged 17
by the greatest band I've ever seen.
From my maddest, baddest, wettest dream,
they were bite me nightly Gutterfuck Queens.
In leather pants and cheap cosmetics.
'Smack addicted fag' aesthetics.
'He-male, female, she-male' dudes
who left the teenage boys confused.
Looking like they fell from Mars
as partial Martian superstars!

Yeah, they put the devil's finest tunes
and killer, thriller attitudes
with every truth you've felt or heard,
to music from another world.
They *mashed* it to a heady brew.
A hoodoo, voodoo guru stew
of Rock&Roll and garage punk,
with Stax of soul and ghetto funk.
And nothing's as fantastic as
iconoclastic spastic jazz
with holy poetry sympathies
and Satan's finest symphonies!

Then it's front page outrage gutterpunk.
But they splattered it with blood and spunk
and sweat and snot and spit and bile
and sprayed it forty thousand miles.
They took a generation's rage
and put it on a tiny stage
and amped it through a speaker stack
and *made the fucking planet crack!*

And yes, it ended in a mess
of drug arrests and early deaths.
And lawsuits over royalties
and madness and disloyalties
and tarnished, varnished trophy wives.
'I used to be somebody' lives.

But that don't mean *a thing* to me.
I close my eyes and I can see
them standing on a tiny stage,
personifying teenage rage.
Pumped up with amphetamine,
and pumping pure adrenaline.
That haunted, howling, shouting face.
The awesome sounding, pounding bass.
That primal, tribal, bible beat
to brain and balls and heart and feet.
That thundered to your very soul
and made your parents' heads explode!

The faces from my bedroom wall.
The faces who would *change it all.*
The guys who'd revolutionise,
liberate, politicise
a total generation's lives.
A legacy that never dies.
From tough estates to trailer parks
they taught us we *should* reach the stars.

And the best thing I was ever shown?
Was 'fuck the rule book – write your own!'

And their message was to liberate,
unite, excite, emancipate
the poor and poorest of this world,
the left out, stressed out boys and girls.
To black and white and straight and gay
they showed there *is* another way.
They taught us that by questioning
together we'll change everything.
And everything we're told is 'theirs'
is there for all the world to share.

So is that unbelievable?
Or something quite conceivable?
Do you find it feasible?
Or something quite unreasonable?
Do you believe that Rock&Roll
can blow the mind and free the soul?
Now it's time to take a poll.
Make some noise for Rock&Roll!
Make some noise for Rock&Roll!
Make some noise for Rock&Roll!

Say, 'I believe!'
Say, 'I believe!'
Say, 'I believe!'

Awopbopaloobopawopbamboom!

KEEPING IT PEEL: TEENAGE KICKER CONSPIRACY

Back in the era when vinyl was vital
Each platter that mattered a vital recital
When the Festive Fifty and every Peel session
Was essential listening, a real obsession
When Peel Acres and Maida Vale
Were secretly famous, a complete Holy Grail
An avancular uncle with a grizzly grey beard
A funky punk uncle still keeping it weird

You were dry and ironic on Top of the Pops
You were wry and sardonic as they bopped 'til they dropped
You would stand there bemused, just extracting the urine
Then, completely amused as you slipped something pure in
And you played the essentials, a playlist of passion
Not the inconsequential with the vagueness of fashion
And we, the outsiders, with music inside us
And Peel the provider, just there to provide us
With weirdness and beardness, the craziest combos
Yes, sometimes you'd fail but you'd fail with aplomb though
And *who cared* that you played them at all the wrong speeds
'Cos you were daring to play them and that's all it needs

And there was Hegley and Joolz, there was Linton KJ
Johnny Clarke and Attila were blazing the way
Ivor Cutler and Swells, and all different wordsmiths
But you'd time for them all so you really deserve this...
You see, music is grateful and they've had chance to show it
But I'd like to say thanks on *behalf of the poets*

And you told us of Walters, The Kop and your wife
While *every night* this DJ was saving my life
And you're missed on the wireless and Glastonbury telly
And it's just not the same without Peel in his wellies
So I just wanna tell you, wanna tell you tonight
And say thanks for the kicks, John, mate, right through the night
Well alright!

WHEN KENDAL CALLS

We've worked all year, we've had to fight
But now we've really earned the right
To party hard into the night
In this beautiful part of the world

We'll leave the stressful world behind
Then we'll successfully unwind
And feel a festival blow our minds
In this beautiful part of the world

We'll bring guitars and glitter balls
We'll bring our art and hearts and all
From near and far when Kendal Calls us
To this beautiful part of the world

We'll drum and basecamp over there
But wear as little as we dare
Just smiles and flowers in our hair
In this beautiful part of the world

We'll laze around, do crazy things
We'll chase around in painted wings
Amaze our soul and make it sing
In this beautiful part of the world

We'll put the funk back into fun
We'll rub-a-dubstep in the sun
We'll rave with lasers set to stun
In this beautiful part of the world

We'll find a stranger, share a kiss
We'll grind to bass lines made of bliss
All kinds of ace times made from this
In this beautiful part of the world

A special smile on every face
For special times, a precious place
We'll leave our hearts but leave no trace
In this beautiful part of the world

So love and laugh as loud guitars
Inspire a choir they'll hear on Mars
To sing our songs beneath the stars
From this beautiful part of the world

And dance at dawn until it breaks!
Until the very mountain shakes!
Until our love fills all the lakes!
And plays…

a beautiful part in this world!

WHY GLASTONBURY

G is for the green fields and for grinning in the queues
L is for that long walk with your luggage and your booze
A is for the atmosphere. It's awesome, always fun
S is for the sunrise. And the sunsets. And the sun
T is for the toilets and the traffic and the tents
O is for outrageous and for Oh! My! God! events
N is for the night-time filled with naughtiness, insane and
B is beer and burgers, bongos banging in your brain and
U is uuuurgh, 'ungover! But you're up until you drop and
R is righteous rock and roll and raving round the clock and
Y could be for youth, it could be yoga in a yurt, but
Y is why they do this, why we come back every year, it's
Y this is a festival with *so much* heart and soul, it's
Y this is a festival with *more* than rock and roll
Why? Because it's built on love! We find it in ourselves
And while we're feeling loved up, we love everybody else
And Greenpeace, Oxfam, Wateraid and all the other causes
Teach that people loving people is the strongest of resources
And so why don't we share lessons from this special time together?
And why don't we ask why *more? Why can't* things change forever?
And so why don't *we* resolve here *now* that Glastonbury's flames
Will light a million beacons and ignite the sparks of change
And so why don't *we* take strength here as a mighty flock of doves?
With a single word to change the world, that simple word is Love!
I said, why don't we grow wings here as a mighty flock of doves?
With a single word to change the world, that simple word is LOVE!
I said, why don't we take flight here as a mighty flock of doves
With a single word to change the world, that simple word is LOVE!
And let's *burn and soar like lanterns*, with a smile on every face
We'll take heart but leave a piece here. It's so hard to leave no trace

And *that's why* there is a part of us
that stays here when we're gone

And *that's why* it's *always* special
in these Fields of Avalon

BLACK JEHOVAH

He was a Jack 'n' Cola Black Jehovah
Whiskey, Kiss-me Casanova
Fuck your soul then roll you over
He'd rock 'n' roll yer!

Looked like he'd take you down and chicken choke yer
Grind your bones then snort and smoke yer
Bet yer soul in a game of poker
A wild card; The Joker.

But when he spoke and when he sang
The words he wrote could rock you, man
He spoke of things that went unsaid
The thoughts that never leave your head
He'd take your deepest hopes and fears and
schemes and dreams and bright ideas and
plans and scams and hidden wounds and
wrap them round his killer tunes

And he held guitars like sacrifices
Tortured them through strange devices
Torched, debauched and slaughtered sounds
He cranked it up and laid it down

A winding, grinding, blinding noise
A million hells, a billion joys
A polyphonic, sonic wave
A manic messianic rave
That soared to an epiphany
Climbed higher beyond ecstasy
And led you gently by the hand
To a frantic tantric promised land
Where your *every fibre* pulsed and burst
To the rhythms of the universe

So when he said that war is wrong
And when he sang a rebel song

And when he took a stand for peace
And when he called for Man's release
And when he started questioning
The status quo and *everything*
And when he challenged privilege
And old school ties and patronage
And when he sang of poverty
And *lies* and rank hypocrisy
And when he said humanity
Shares rainbow sexuality
And when he said the media
Should stop the shit they feed to yer
And when he said that monarchy
Is mocking our democracy
And when he said our governance
Is money men, not governments
And when he said that black and white
Should find a common cause to fight
And when he said that 'Love Is All'
Should be the only battle call

Well, then they saw his prophecies
Were launching new philosophies
And then they saw this preacher man
Could reach and teach his fellow man
And then they saw the way his news
Could sway the way *the world* is viewed
And then they saw his images
Could *burn* their craven effigies
And then they saw guitars and lines
Could win the war for hearts and minds
And then they saw that strings and rhymes
Could shift their shitty paradigms
And then they saw his tunes and chords
Could down our tools and stop their wars
And then they saw that 'Love Is All'
Filled *every* teenage bedroom wall

And then they saw him energise
The powerless and paralysed
And once they were politicised
He showed them how to organize
So when they saw their plans were *rrrrocked*

They framed a man

and had him shot

He was a Jack 'n' Cola Black Jehovah
Whiskey, Kiss-me Casanova
Seek his words and think them over
He fuckin' showed yer

Peace

It's a great tattoo.
But I said 'Joy Division.'
Not 'Jim Davidson.'

In the 'Ten Items
Or Less' queue with twelve items
thinking: *Punk's Not Dead!*

'When the power of love overcomes the love of power,
then the world will know peace.'
Jimi Hendrix

TRASH PLANET

Welcome!

To a grown up world of garages
Of happy slappy marriages
Of loans and lawns and mortgage forms
Abortions and miscarriages
And toothless jukebox jiving fans
And skiving fans with driving bans
And pool shark card sharp ne'er-do-wells
With smoky bacon armpit smells

On sugar fat salt sugar diets
On sugar fat salt sugar diets
On sugar fat salt sugar diets
On Trash Planet, Trash Planet

And check out all the checkout queues
Where chip and pinned down checkout crews
Help arsehole APR- sold fans
Spend never-read-it credit plans
And max-out all our debit cards
To bail out all our credit cards
And race rats on the rat race wheels
To high VAT, high fat meal deals

On sugar fat salt sugar diets
On sugar fat salt sugar diets
On sugar fat salt sugar diets
On Trash Planet, Trash Planet

And surf around the internet
For friends you've not had sex with yet
Have cyber sex on CyberHo
Dotcom. (They're blokes from Idaho!)
And when you've had your cyber-wank
Just pop down to the Girobank
And spunk your cash on lotteries
And Harley Street lobotomies

On sugar fat salt sugar diets
On sugar fat salt sugar diets
On sugar fat salt sugar diets
On Trash Planet, Trash Planet

And keep your brand demands all scanned
And keep your white skin perma-tanned
Buy skincare swimwear diet plans
For Champagne Melanoma fans
Then fish around with microchips
For resale retail credit slips
And clone a cloned identity
And buy yourself celebrity

On sugar fat salt sugar diets
On sugar fat salt sugar diets
On sugar fat salt sugar diets
On Trash Planet, Trash Planet

Then fall from cars in push-up bras
And fight in bars with fucked-up stars
Then snap at paparazzi lest
They Molotov your cocktail dress
Or join the happy taxi queues
The thrown up, blown up, grown up blues
Of ketchup, punch up, dog shish riots
On sugar fat salt sugar diets

On sugar fat salt sugar diets
On sugar fat salt sugar diets
On sugar fat salt sugar diets
On Trash Planet, Trash Planet
Trash Planet, Trash Planet
Trash Planet, Trash Planet
STOP!

T-SHIRT PHILOSOPHY

Lenin and Presley
Lennon and Trotsky
Jagger and Jesus
Mao and Monroe

Bolan and Castro
Hitler and Ringo
Evita and Tito
Malcolm X, Jackie O

Cobain and Coltrane
Bobbit and John Wayne
Rotten and Reagan
Pele and Slash

Kylie, Selassie
Smiley and Bassey
Madonna, Mandela
Beckham and Cash

Clinton and Clapton
Dylan and Nixon
Hendrix and Heston
Bowie and Dean

Dali and Marley
Diana and Charlie
Rushdie, Gadaffi
Ali, Amin

Jackson and Tyson
Hoover and Dyson
Ghandi and Britney
Kilroy and Keane

Saddam, Sinatra
Stalin, Garfunkel
Molotov, Thatcher
Vicious, The Queen

SUGAR SPUN TORNADOES

And *he* believes that God believes in rock and roll and rainbows
And *she* believes that candyfloss is sugar spun tornadoes
And *he* believes that Jesus bleeds the red in stained glass windows
And *I* believe in dreaming dreams and I *have* a dream!

And she believes in bumblebees and birds and karma sutra
And he believes that dragon flies bring memories from the future
And she believes that babies' eyes are love guns and they shoot ya
And I believe in dreaming dreams and I have a dream!

And she believes that poetry and poverty are sisters
And he believes that rocking chairs are dynamos for twisters
And she believes that gasoline is piss from Satan's blisters
And I believe in dreaming dreams and I have a dream!

And he believes that unicorns are ghosts from Noah's stables
And she believes that crop circles are landing strips for angels
And he believes he'll bomb himself a place at heaven's tables
And I believe in dreaming dreams and I have a dream!

And he believes Kalashnikov should ride on Lenin's shoulders
And she believes that fireflies are spies from supernovas
And he believes the desert's made from dried and powdered soldiers
And I believe in dreaming dreams and I have a dream!

And she believes the summer breeze is just Jehovah breathing
And he believes when mushroom clouds Beelzebub is sneezing
And she believes when lava flows that mother earth is bleeding
And I believe in dreaming dreams and I have a dream!

And she believes that poppy seeds can grow into solutions
And he believes that record sleeves can lead to revolutions
And she believes that counting beads can lead to absolutions
And I believe in dreaming dreams and I have a dream!

And he believes that camels can still fit through tiny needles
And she believes that moneylenders kneel and weep for Jesus

And he believes in *knocking nails* through those that would deceive us
And I believe in dreaming dreams and I have a dream!

And I believe that soda pop is sugar mixed with warfare
And I believe we need to drop some stealth bombs into healthcare
And I believe we need to turn our wealth into our welfare
And I believe in dreaming dreams and I have a dream!

And I believe the planet, if we plan it, *can* sustain us
And I believe that prophets do not profit but detain us
And I believe their shackles if they're tackled *can't contain us*
And I believe in dreaming dreams and I have a dream!

And I believe in cluster bombs – of peace and hope and caring
And I believe we *can* achieve the shock and awe of sharing
And I believe that spreading love should win awards for daring
Yeah, *I* believe in dreaming dreams!
Do *you* believe in dreaming dreams?
Can *we* believe in dreaming dreams?
I have a dream!

NEAT LAWNS (NOW WATCH THIS DRIVE)

And when the bell tolls
in the hell holes
and the poor people die.
Does it meet yawns
from the neat lawns
where the rich people lie?

And when the shots hail
and the crops fail
and the poor people die.
Could they care less?
Could they share less
where the rich people lie?

And when the healthcare
is sent elsewhere
and the poor people die.
Is a price paid?
Is a life saved
where the rich people lie?

And in the earthquakes
when the earth shakes
and the poor people die.
Is their worth proved?
Does the earth move
where the rich people lie?

And when the seas rise,
when disease thrives
and the poor people die.
Is their pain felt?
Is there shame felt
where the rich people lie?

And when the wars blaze
and the wars rage

and the poor people die.
Are their pleas heard?
Are their screams heard
where the rich people lie?

And for the vast waves
in the mass graves
when the poor people die.
Do they dwell long?
Is the smell strong
where the rich people lie?

And in the death throes
on the death rows
when the poor people *fry*.
Does the power trail
make the power fail
where the rich people lie?

And in the sweat shops
and the death blocks
where the poor people die.
Is the truth shown?
Is the truth known
where the rich people lie?

And when we seek truth
do we meet truth?
Why *do* poor people die?
Is it treason?
Or the reason
to say 'rich

people

lie?'

REPEAT AFTER ME

Number one	Sleep as long as you like – just be awake more
Number two	See through their mirrors and truly reflect
Number three	Every day should end in Y and begin with 'Why Not?'
Number four	Understand that happiness is more important than pleasure
Number five	Judge a philosophy by its best teachings – not by its worst students
Number six	Know this: we are all foreigners in most places
Number seven	Treat people differently that they may be equal
Number eight	Buy less and spend more time
Number nine	Walk more and leave smaller footprints
Number ten	Don't die of consumption
Number eleven	Don't make poverty history – make it current affairs
Number twelve	Save seeds from flowers
Number thirteen	Grow flowers from seeds
Number fourteen	Understand the glory of nature and the nature of glory
Number fifteen	Learn the answers and teach the questions
Number sixteen	Give big dreams to small children

Number seventeen	Smile more
Number eighteen	Dance more
Number nineteen	Touch people
Number twenty	Be a good kisser!
Number twenty one	Make love more

Make love more, make love more, make love
more, make love more,
Make love more, make love more, make love
more

Make love more...

prevalent in the world

BECAUSE THE POETS KNOW

Because the poets know
Because the poets feel
Because the poets understand
Because the poets think
Because the poets see
Because the poets take a stand

Because the poets move
Because the poets stir
Because the poets write it down
Because the poets blaze
Because the poets rage
Because the poets say it loud

And some may abhor us
And some just ignore us
And sometimes we suffer slings
But sometimes they laud us
And some lands applaud us
And sometimes they crown us kings

But some raid our stages
And some burn our pages
And some throw us into cells
And sometimes they tape us
And sometimes they rape us
And some die in living hells

And sometimes we're banished
And sometimes we're vanished
And some drive us from our lands
And some persecute us
And some execute us
And some chop off poets' hands

And sometimes we're tortured
And sometimes we're slaughtered

And some cut out poets' tongues
But *sometimes* they hear us
And *sometimes* they cheer us
And *sometimes* they sing our songs

Because the poets know
Because the poets feel
Because the poets understand
Because the poets think
Because the poets see
Because the poets take a stand

Because the poets move
Because the poets stir
Because the poets write it down
Because the poets blaze
Because the poets rage
Because the poets say it loud

If *you* are a poet
If *I* am a poet
If *we* are all poets, say loud:

'Your pressure and violence
will beat neither silence
nor soul from a poet.'

Stand proud!

THE HIGHEST HILL

Climb the highest hill
and start a fire
for hope.

Climb the highest hill
and start a fire
for peace.

Climb the highest hill
and start a fire
for Earth.

Climb the highest hill
and start a fire
for love.

Build
the highest hill

from promises,
pledges,
manifestos,
charters,
balance sheets,
maps
and scriptures.

Climb the highest hill

AND START A FIRE!

TAKE THIS PEN

Ok, this poem goes out to all the wonderful young poets out there.
To everyone who thinks that poetry is not for you,
and to everyone who knows that it really, really is.
It's called Take This Pen,
and it goes like this…

To the kid they pick on, 'cos you're small.
The kid they kick because you're tall.
The kid they trip to watch you fall.
Poetry is *for* you. It's *for* you!

To the kid who's anxious, every day.
The last kid, when they're picked to play.
The quiet kid with lots to say.
Poetry is *for* you.

To the kid who hides behind their hair.
Who's scared and scarred by every stare.
The kid who cries when no-one's there.
Poetry is *for* you.

To the kid that no-one sees or hears.
The kid who knows she'll end up pierced
to drain the pain of tattooed tears.
Poetry is *for* you.

To the girl who's never, ever sure
or confident, but knows she's poor.
And knows *there must* be something more.
Poetry is *for* you.

To the lad whose dad is always missed.
The kid whose mum is always pissed.
The girl with scratch marks on her wrist.
Poetry is *for* you.

To the kid not wired to follow rules.
The kid hot-wired to glow, so fools
exclude you from deluded schools and
poetry is *for* you.

152

To the kid who won't buy what we're sold.
The kid who questions what we're told.
You're a treasure chest of buried gold and
poetry is *for* you.

To the kid who feels they don't belong,
that nothing's right, that something's wrong.
But to carry weakness makes you strong so
poetry is *for* you.

To the girl whose birth was overseas.
She burns and yearns to learn so she's
collecting words like a bunch of keys.
Poetry is *for* you!

To the kid who sees that reading breeds
deep feelings for his people's needs,
so he reads and reads and reads and reads.
Poetry is *for* you

To the kid who knows that light can bring
out rainbows on a magpie's wings.
Pens song words when the songbird sings.
Poetry is *for* you.

To the kid who's never seen the sea,
but floats across the oceans, free
in dreamboats from the library.
Poetry is *for* you.

To the kid who cries for rides in cars,
but flies inside astride the stars,
finds diamond rhymes in the mines of Mars!
Poetry is *for* you.

To the kid they always call a freak,
a nerd, a wuss, a swot, a geek,
a weirdo, but you're you! Unique and
poetry is *for* you

To that kid inside now! Fully grown.
But you still feel – somehow – on your own.
Join us. Cos you're not alone and
poetry is *for* you.

Welcome! We're expecting you!
We've saved a place for you. It's true
that you are us and we are you and
poetry is *for* you.

You're different. But we're the same!
Strange family, all with different names.
But we're all lit from a single flame.
And poetry is *for* you.

So here's a gift to you from me;
the pen a poet gave to me.
Take it. It will set you free.
And poetry is *for* you.

Now prick your finger, take this pen and
dip it in your blood and then you
turn your burn to nine then Zen and
poetry is *for* you.

Then lift the gift that nature gave
with graft and craft, re-draft and slave
for greatness. It awaits the brave when
poetry is *for* you

So turn every tear you've ever wept,
and every jeer you've ever kept,
and every fear you've never slept into
poetry that's *for* you

And think of all those stutter times,
those mutter in the gutter times.
Then put it in and utter lines like
poetry is *for* you.

And scribe in blood and flood the page and
stride with pride across the stage and
spit it in a fit of rage that
poetry is *for* you!

And you're NOT that shy kid anymore and
THIS is what you're waiting for!
You're so much, so much, SO MUCH MORE!
And poetry is *for* you!

A giant now! No longer small!
And no-one's laughing 'cos you're tall.
From up here you can see it all!
And poetry is *for* you!

So grab the mic now, face the crowd and
tell them loud how you have vowed
to leave them wowed and how you're proud that
poetry is *for* you.

And be brilliant and unbreakable.
Distinct and unmistakable.
Unsinkable, unshakeable.
Now poetry is *for* you.

And be brave and confrontational.
Inspired and inspirational.
Unafraid to be sensational!
Now poetry is *for* you.

And even if they criticize,
believe and don't apologize.
The foolish always mock the wise.
And poetry is *for* you!

But our craft outlasts their nasty games.
Their laughter only fans our flames.
And forgotten hands carve poets' names when
poetry is *for* you.

So we fight *because* it's frightening.
Writer's duty? Be exciting!
See the beauty! Free the lightning!
Now poetry is *for* you.

So never, ever, *ever* fear and
keep the flame in *here* and *here* and
shine your light and make it clear
that poetry is *for* you.

And search for more, along the way.
The lost ones that you'll find some day.
Just look into their eyes and say
that poetry is *for* you.

Then say, 'Here's a gift to you from me;
the pen a poet gave to me.
Take it. It will set you free.
And poetry is *for* you.'

And there's easier ways to spend your days.
Huh, Jesus! Let me count the ways!
But if you… *shiver*… when a poet says
that poetry is *for* you. It's *for* you!
It's *for* you.
It's *for* you.

THE LAST GANG IN TOWN?

Who, these days, are the rebels worth the name?
Who hates the army, hates the RAF?
Who, these days, takes a gutter sniper's aim?
Who fights the law with every beat and breath?

Who, these days, has the baselines or the balls?
Who's sussed and struts where white man fears to tread?
Who, these days, answers back when London calls?
Who catches fire and burns like Natty Dread?

Who'll wave a flag above the shit parade?
Who'll educate and agitate the youth?
Who'll use guitars as weapons, unafraid?
Who'll rock the very casbah with the truth?

Come, stand and fight; together, not alone.
Go, start a fucking riot of your own.

'Stand before the people you fear and speak your mind;
even if your voice shakes.'
Maggie Kuhn

NOTES

Too Much Poetry – a version of this poem was first published in The Ugly Tree, issue 17, Flapjack Press, 2008.

The Poetry Slam Prayer – arose from an Apples & Snakes competition to write them a new slogan. Four lines from this poem won the competition and featured in promotional materials around 2008.

Start All The Clocks – I'd love to use this piece in poetry slam competitions. Frustratingly, however, it exceeds the permitted three minutes running time.

Drastic Surgery – was published in The Ugly Tree, Flapjack Press, issue 4, 2004. It was also published in 2004 by Lime Arts in their Echoes Down Corridors project alongside an image of LS Lowry's 1952 painting, Ancoats Hospital Outpatients' Hall. The poem, like several here, was written around 2002 when I was living and working in the most deprived wards of Manchester and Salford.

It's All Going Posh Down The Precinct – was written around 2004 in the voice of an older man who feels excluded by the inner-city regeneration and gentrification going on around him.

A Girl, Like, Y'Know – was written in 2004 in the voice of a young woman aged 16 or 17. A favourite from my live set, a video of me performing the piece can be found on YouTube, filmed by Richard Davis in 2011.

No Walls – was published in a 2005 edition of Citizen32, as well as in Doing December Differently: An Alternative Christmas Handbook, Wild Goose Publications, 2006.

Saving Deposits – was first published in Citizen32, 2005.

No Mark – is a Scouse insult used to call someone worthless. The phrase echoes a line from Shakespeare's Henry IV Part 1: 'A fellow of no mark nor likelihood.'

Tiny Dreams – shares a few lines with my poem, Binbags, first published in the anthology, Home, UCLAN Press, 2007.

Ho! Ho! Ho! – was inspired by a black and white photo of my four year old self looking forlorn with a tatty and equally forlorn looking Father Christmas.

Battered – was first published in the anthology, Taste, UCLAN Press, 2006.

Someone Warm To Hold – was written for a 2007 tour called Love v Lust. We did 7 nights around the north west of England for this Commonword-led project, the most memorable of which was in Styal women's prison. The show took the form of two teams, each with three poets, debating the issues in poetry. The audience used voting cards to determine the winning team each night. The Love team, for which this poem was the closing argument, won 7-0.

Intimacy – when reading this poem live I often interrupt myself and ask the audience to help me choose a less harsh, more playful word for the male sexual organ, with often amusing results. First published in Citizen32, 2006.

I Can Write A Rainbow – the line about 'another name for thesaurus,' references a joke originally made by deadpan US comedian, Steven Wright. Film-maker Christine Flannery's 2009 re-interpretation of the poem for Comma Film/Version Film Festival can be found on YouTube. In Christine's film the poem ceases to be a writer talking to their lover and becomes a small child talking to their mother.

Three Wishes – was written for my sister's registry office wedding. However, in the end, I wasn't allowed to use it as the registrar ruled it out on the grounds of its Biblical reference (John 19:40). The line 'spice me like Christ' refers to the Jewish burial practice of wrapping a body in strips of linen soaked in spices, which struck me as a particularly loving and tender act.

Nothing New – came from an idea which I sat on for about 10 years, from when we first had children. I'd learnt about this hitherto mysterious aisle in the supermarket and imagined a woman who became upset each week when she has to walk past it.

Cake Hole – is based on a true story. It seemed that the Tooth Fairy had forgotten to call at our house one morning. We were able to explain however that, having risen early, we were simply up before she had managed to reach homes such as ours where the child's surname begins with W.

Happy Meals – was first published in the anthology, Taste, UCLAN Press, 2006.

Mother's Day – was inspired by a conversation with Eric Allison, prison correspondent for The Guardian newspaper. Eric told me that levels of suicide and self-harm peak in women's prisons around Mother's Day and the poem is my reflection on the many reasons why.

Sometimes – was made into a moving and award-winning short film directed by David Wharton and starring James Foster (Coronation Street, Cold Feet, etc). It won first prize at Version Film Festival at Manchester's Cornerhouse arts centre and was subsequently screened at short film festivals around the UK, including Aesthetica and

Branchage, as well as at Magma International Short Film Festival in Sicily and The Body Electric Poetry Film Festival in Colorado, USA. The film can be found online on Vimeo and via my website.

Don't Waste Your Breath – was a Poem of the Month on Apples & Snakes' website in around 2007.

Smoke Lonely – the text and an audio recording of this poem first appeared on the website for StAnza: Scotland's International Poetry Festival prior to my appearance there in 2011.

Cherry Blossom – is a UK brand of shoe polish which comes in those small flat tins. The poem came to me as I was cleaning my shoes for the funeral of much missed Manchester poet, Dike Omeje. First published in The Ugly Tree, issue 20, 2009.

Always There – I was interested in how the tiny linguistic change of 'a he caring for a he' changes the politics of the poem so dramatically from 'a she caring for a he' and other permutations. To my mind the poem isn't necessarily about HIV/AIDS as many people assume, but I remain humbled by how much the poem continues to move many audiences. The poem was originally written for the Love v Lust tour, see above.

Life Goes On – is the poem that I wrote to read at my mother's funeral. To me it's a science-based, atheist poem, but it can also be interpreted to be about a God's omnipresence, it seems. My brother and his wife are both church ministers and so there were a dozen or more ministers in the church when I read this.

Special Place – was written as a poem, but also turned itself into a song. The musical fade-out – in my head, at least – has the sort of transcendent ending to which the lyric refers.

Rock&Roll – to answer the many people who ask me, imagines a fictional, hybrid band which comprises of: the other-worldly fashion of 70s-era Rolling Stones, Bowie and the New York Dolls; the incendiary politics of The MC5 and The Clash; the sonic assault of Iggy and the Stooges; and the unparalleled cultural impact of the Sex Pistols. I'm sure that bands like Manic Street Preachers and my beloved Jesus and Mary Chain are in there somewhere also. The 'blood and spunk' line is a reference to an NME article about Placebo. Written around 2005, the poem was first published in the USA anthology, Punk Rock Saved My Ass, Medusa's Muse press, 2010.

Keeping It Peel: Teenage Kicker Conspiracy – was written on-site at the Glastonbury Festival of Contemporary Performing Arts 2011, where I held the post of website Poet in Residence. I performed the poem on Cerys Matthews' show on BBC6Music live from the festival and

twice, subsequently on Jo Whiley's show on BBC Radio 2. First published in Scribble magazine, Cartwheel Arts, 2012.
When Kendal Calls – was written in 2012 as part of my role as Poet Laureate for the Kendal Calling Festival in England's beautiful Lake District. I met Debbie Harry at Kendal Calling 2011, but that's another story...
Why Glastonbury – featured in the 2011 official end-of-festival thank you message. My audio of the poem, accompanied by Rohan Van Twest's excellent photographs, can be found on YouTube where it has clocked up over 11,000 hits.
Sugar Spun Tornadoes – featured in Burning Eye's 2013 e-book, West of Centre: A Taste of Burning Eye.
Neat Lawns (Now Watch This Drive) – the sub-title refers to the famous quote from George W Bush who was filmed playing golf, and carrying on regardless, when discussing terrorism after the 9/11 attacks.
Repeat After Me – has sometimes gone under the alternative title of New Year Revolutions and can be found online under that title, in a text-art collaboration with Paolo Feroleto.
Because The Poets Know – was published in 2012 by EnglishPEN and also translated into Russian as part of their Catechism: Poems For Pussy Riot anthology, e-book and campaign.
The Highest Hill – began life in a traffic jam approaching my first Glastonbury Festival in 2005, snaking past Glastonbury Tor.
The Last Gang In Town? – is a Shakespearean sonnet about The Clash, to be published in Double Bill, the sequel to Split Screen (Red Squirrel Press). I liked the idea of using the discipline of the 14 line formal sonnet (meaning 'little song') to eulogise a disciplined, principled band with short, sharp songs. Many of the lines and the title are references to Clash lyrics. I did a video on YouTube for this poem with thespeakerscorner.co.uk which Billy Bragg shared on Facebook, calling it, 'a call to arms for young bands.'
Haiku – Several of the haiku included here were first published in Manchester listings magazine, 80:20. Strictly speaking, most of the 'haiku' here are actually in the lesser known 'senryū' form. All are 17 syllables or fewer, not all adopt the 5-7-5 structure if this better serves the meaning of the piece.

OTHER POETS ARE ALSO AVAILABLE

I've seen 95% of these excellent poets and spoken word artists, and heard good things about all of them. They represent a huge range of voices, styles and profiles, and are listed here in no particular order; the only order being to check them out – on line, on the page and on a stage near you.

John Hegley ǀ Ian McMillan ǀ Roger McGough ǀ John Cooper Clarke ǀ Jean 'Binta' Breeze ǀ Linton Kwesi Johnson ǀ Lemn Sissay ǀ Benjamin Zephaniah ǀ Ivor Cutler (RIP) ǀ Murray Lachlan Young ǀ Joolz Denby ǀ Tony Harrison ǀ Attila the Stockbroker ǀ Gerry Potter ǀ Chloe Poems ǀ Ben Mellor ǀ Jackie Hagan ǀ Ali Gadema ǀ Dominic Berry ǀ Rosie Garland ǀ Mike Garry ǀ Jo Bell ǀ Working Verse Collective ǀ Alabaster DePlume ǀ Amanda Milligan ǀ Shirley May ǀ Young Identity collective ǀ Monkey Poet ǀ Hovis Presley (RIP) ǀ Dike Omeje (RIP) ǀ Marvin Cheeseman ǀ Mark Mace Smith ǀ Segun Lee French ǀ Tony Curry ǀ Conor Aylward ǀ Paul Neads ǀ Steve O'Connor ǀ Charlotte Henson ǀ Martin Stannage (aka Visceral) ǀ Michelle Green ǀ Rod Tame ǀ Steph Pike ǀ Joy France ǀ Chanje Kunda ǀ Emma Decent ǀ Thick Richard ǀ Helen Clare ǀ Shamshad Khan ǀ John G Hall ǀ Gemma Lees ǀ Anjum Malik ǀ Julian Jordon ǀ Dave Morgan ǀ Nat Clare ǀ Jeffarama ǀ Scott Devon ǀ Gordon Zola ǀ Yusra Warsama ǀ Polarbear ǀ Inua Ellams ǀ David J ǀ Kate Tempest ǀ Scroobius Pip ǀ Vanessa Kisuule ǀ Dan Cockrill ǀ Jacob Sam- La Rose ǀ Elvis McGonagall ǀ Joshua Idehen ǀ Rob Auton ǀ Mista Gee ǀ Zena Edwards ǀ Malika Booker ǀ Kat Francois ǀ Adam Kammerling ǀ Rosy Carrick ǀ Patience Agbabi ǀ Nii Ayikwei Parkes ǀ Simon Mole ǀ Dennis Just Dennis ǀ Dean Atta ǀ Max Wallis ǀ Hollie McNish ǀ Catherine Brogan ǀ Pete The Temp ǀ Joelle Taylor ǀ Paula Varjack ǀ Poeticat ǀ Angry Sam ǀ Ash Dickinson ǀ Julian Daniel ǀ John Paul O'Neill ǀ Phenzwaan ǀRachel Pantechnicon ǀ Anthony Anaxagorou ǀ George Chopping ǀ Kayo Chingonyi ǀ Joe Kriss ǀ Tim Wells ǀ Anna Le ǀ Aisle 16 ǀ Luke Wright ǀ Tim Clare ǀ Ross Sutherland ǀ John Osborne ǀ Joe Dunthorne ǀ Joel Stickley ǀ Molly Naylor ǀ Martin Figura ǀ Pete Hunter ǀ Michelle Madsen ǀ Salena Godden ǀ Peter Hayhoe ǀ Martin Galton ǀ Francesca Beard ǀ Mark Gwynne Jones ǀ Charlie Dark ǀ Nathan Penlington ǀ Matt Harvey ǀ Dzifa Benson ǀ The Anti-Poet ǀ Chris Redmond ǀ Katie Bonna ǀ Rachel Rose Reid ǀ Dan Simpson ǀ Mel Jones ǀ Sabrina Mahfouz ǀ Porky the Poet ǀ Lowkey ǀ David Lee Morgan ǀ Raymond Antrobus ǀ

Laura Dockrill | Sophia Blackwell | George The Poet | Brenda Read-Brown | Peter Wyton | Kim Trusty | Andrew McMillan | Andy Willoughby | Claire Murphy Morgan | Alison Brumfitt | Maxwell Golden |Dreadlockalien | Spoz | Charlie Jordan | Matt 'Man' Windle | Bohdan Piasecki | Nick Toczek | Paul Cookson | Terry Caffrey | Helen Mort | Richard Tyrone Jones | Mark Grist | Jodi Ann Bickley | Mab Jones | Rob Gee | Harry Baker |Niall O'Sullivan | Jonny Fluffypunk | Annie McGann | Lucy English | Aoife Mannix | Rhian Edwards | Al Cummins | Byron Vincent | Liz Greenfield | Wilf Mertens | Nathan Filer | Sally Jenkinson | Anna Freeman | AF Harrold | Clare Kirwan | David Bateman | Cath Nichols | Jason Richardson | Martin Daws | Ann The Poet | Emma McGordon | Kim Moore| Jenny Lindsay | Rachel McCrum | Robin Cairns | Sara Jane Arbury | Marcus Moore | Mark Niel | Toby Thompson | Helen Gregory | Dizraeli | Steve Larkin | Spliff Richard | Stephen James Smith | Colm Keegan | Kalle Ryan | Chelley McLear | Abby Oliveira | Pamela Brown | The Poetry Chicks | Marty Mulligan | Erin Fornoff | Andy Craven Griffiths | John Berkavitch | Joe Hakim | Mike Watts | Kate Fox | Poetry Jack | Scott Tyrell | Jenni Pascoe | Hannah Silva | Steve Rooney | Rachael Black | Jeff Price | John Siddique | Sarah Thomasin | MC Angel | The Ruby Kid | Shane Koyczan | Patti Smith | Mike McGee | Saul Williams | Buddy Wakefield | Taylor Mali | Sarah Kay | Baba Israel | Ian Keteku | Brad Morden | The Fugitives | CR Avery | Anis Mojgani | Derrick Brown | Baba Brinkman | Penny Ashton | Anthony Joseph | Musa Okwonga | Henry Bowers | Andreattah Chuma | Lisa Baird | Adam Horovitz |Julian Ramsey-Wade | Matt McAteer | The Last Poets | You? | and many more.

http://www.applesandsnakes.org/
http://www.writeoutloud.net
http://www.poetrysociety.org.uk/
http://slam.poetrysociety.org.uk/
http://www.shakethedust.co.uk/
http://wearepoets.co.uk/
http://www.poetrylibrary.org.uk/
http://www.nuyorican.org/

Please note that a listing above implies no endorsement of my own poetry or opinions. My apologies go to those I may have accidentally omitted and to those who feel they should be included. I will keep an updated list online. Do please let me know of names to include.

Lightning Source UK Ltd.
Milton Keynes UK
UKOW04f1322250717
306005UK00001B/153/P